Walking Cheshire's
Sandstone Trail

Looking out from Bickerton Hill, on Cheshire's Sandstone Trail

Walking Cheshire's
Sandstone Trail

*The finest and most popular
middle-distance walk
in Northwest England*

A 55 kilometre/34 mile walk from
Frodsham to **Whitchurch**, along Cheshire's beautiful
and varied central sandstone ridge

Tony Bowerman

Northern Eye

www.**northerneyebooks**.co.uk
www.**sandstonetrail**.co.uk

First published in 2008
New edition 2013
Reprinted 2016, 2017 & 2019
New revised edition 2024

Northern Eye Books
*High Street, Tattenhall,
Cheshire CH3 9PX*

Copyright © Tony Bowerman 2019-2024

Tony Bowerman has asserted his right under the Copyright, Designs and Patents Act, 1988 to be identified as the author of this work. All rights reserved.

ISBN 978-1-908632-33-3

A CIP catalogue record for this book is available from the British Library.

Whilst every effort has been made to ensure that the information in this book is correct at the time of publication, neither the author nor the publisher can accept any responsibility for any errors, loss or injury, however caused.

The routes described in this book are undertaken at the individual's own risk. The publisher and copyright owners accept no responsibility for any consequences arising from the use of this book, including misinterpretation of the maps and directions.

This book contains mapping data licensed from the Ordnance Survey with the permission of the Controller of Her Majesty's Stationery Office.

© Crown copyright 2019-2024. All rights reserved. Licence number 100047867

Acknowledgements

This book could not, of course, have been written without the generous help of many people. Firstly, our heartfelt thanks to John Street, the Sandstone Trail Ranger, for his positive, enthusiastic and unstinting help and advice, and for the use of his many superb photographs. Warm thanks, too, are due to: Jo Danson, of the Countryside Management Service; Alan Bowring, from the Countryside and Rights of Way Office; Alun Evans, from 'Regeneration'; Ellie Soper, Sandstone Ridge ECOnet Partnership Project Officer; the 'Revealing the Past' team and the County Historic Environment Record team; Joe Wainwright, from the Tourism Department—all of Cheshire County Council; Chris Widger and Dave Morris of The National Trust; Cheshire and Chester Archives and Local Studies Service; Chester Reference Library; Chester Archaeological Society; Sue Hughes and the Grosvenor Museum, Chester; Manchester Museum/ the University of Manchester; Helen Bate and the Peckforton Hills Local Heritage Initiative; Pam Hall and the Frodsham & District Local History Society; the Woodland Trust; Landlife; the Whitchurch Waterway Trust; Ginette Hanson, of the Blue Bell Inn at Bell o' th' Hill, Tushingham; and Tom R Wright, of Oakmere. Many thanks, too, to Neil Rogers and Bob Nash for checking the route, and pointing out things we'd overlooked.

Photographs

Photographs copyright © 2006-2024: John Street, Joe Wainwright, Clint Hughes/Cheshire West and Chester Council; Shutterstock; Chester and Cheshire Archives and Local Studies Service; Helen Bate/Peckforton Hills Local Heritage Initiative; Dave Morris/The National Trust; Frodsham History Society; Damian Young/ Landlife; Chester Archaeological Society; Manchester Museum/University of Manchester; Grosvenor Museum/Chester City Council; Ginette Hanson/Blue Bell Inn at Bell o' the Hill, Tushingham; Captain Gordon Fergusson/Tarporley Hunt Club; Patrick Turnbull/ Whitchurch Waterway Trust; Tom Wright, Oakmere; Jean Green, Tiverton; Carl Rogers; Tony Bowerman.
Wildlife photographs: Simon Booth/www.simonboothphotography.com; Damian Waters/ www.drumimages.co.uk; Nigel Fairclough/www.nigelfairclough.co.uk; Peter Smith; John Street.

The publishers have credited pictures wherever possible and sincerely apologise for any unintentional omissions.

Illustration: Background artwork, Roger Stephens.

Contents

Where is the Sandstone Trail 6

The Best of Cheshire 8

Walking Cheshire's Sandstone Trail 10
- Factfile 10
- Origins of the Trail 10
- What is it like? 11
- Using the Trail 11
- Maps 13
- Accommodation 13
- Connecting routes 14

Making sense of the Sandstone Trail 15

Sandstone Trail: Route Directions 35
- **Section 1:** Frodsham to Manley Common 36
- **Section 2:** Manley Common to Gresty's Waste 48
- Exploring Delamere Forest 52
- **Section 3:** Gresty's Waste to Tarporley 60
- **Section 4:** Tarporley to Burwardsley 72
- Exploring Beeston Castle 86
- **Section 5:** Burwardsley to Larkton Hall 88
- **Section 6:** Larkton Hall to Willeymoor Lock 104
- **Section 7:** Willeymoor Lock to Whitchurch 120

Useful Information and website 128

Where is the **Sandstone Trail?**

The **Sandstone Trail** runs roughly north to south through the centre of the lovely—and still largely rural—county of Cheshire, in northwest England.

Morning magic *Beeston Castle at sunrise*

*Walking Cheshire's **Sandstone Trail** 7*

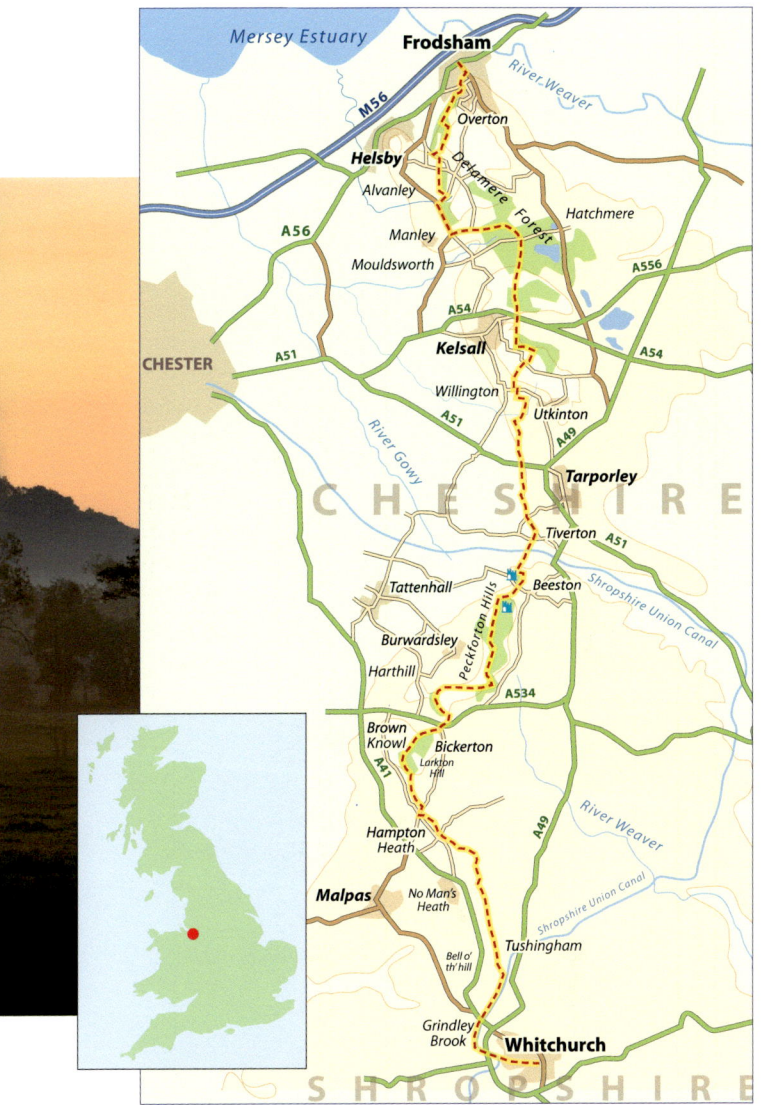

Sandstone Trail: *Cheshire's Sandstone Trail stretches from Frodsham to Whitchurch*

The Best of **Cheshire**

Cheshire's Sandstone Trail is arguably the finest and best loved middle-distance walk in Northwest England. The Trail follows the elevated ridge of sandstone hills—that rise dramatically above the Cheshire Plain—for 55 kilometres/34 miles across this essentially green county, from the broad Mersey estuary to rural north Shropshire.

Along the way you'll experience the very best of Cheshire: everchanging views and lofty panoramas over Wales and the Pennines; wooded escarpments, sandstone cliffs, viewpoints and caves; undulating, oak-dotted pastures and farmland; vast and ancient, sun-dappled Delamere Forest; prehistoric hillforts, dramatic medieval and Victorian castles; half-timbered black-and-white and sandstone manor houses, farms and historic inns; Roman roads, sunken green lanes, packhorse routes, saltways, and old coach roads; tranquil rivers, streams and rural canals; mosses and meres; heathland and heather.

Unspoilt Cheshire is bursting with wild flowers and wildlife, too. Along the Trail can be seen everything from bluebells and bilberries, to buzzards and barn owls, brown hares and butterflies.

Whatever the weather or the season, the Sandstone Trail is a real breath of fresh air.

"The Sandstone Trail is an easy, well signposted, three day family walk with a variety of terrain and wonderful views. We highly recommend it."

Hugh Baker

(son of Jack Baker, who devised the Sandstone Trail)

Walking Cheshire's **Sandstone Trail**

> **FACTFILE**
>
> **Start/Finish**: The Sandstone Trail runs roughly north-south across Cheshire and northern Shropshire between Frodsham and Whitchurch.
>
> **Length**: 34 miles/55 kilometres.
>
> **Difficulty**: The Trail varies in difficulty from easy to moderate, depending on the terrain. Short, steep sections include those at Frodsham, Beeston Castle, Higher Burwardsley, Rawhead and Bickerton. The easiest, flattest sections are those in Delamere Forest Park and alongside the canal between Willeymoor Lock and Whitchurch.
>
> **Terrain**: Wooded sandstone ridge, open woodland and forest, green lanes, lowland heath, undulating farmland, canal towpath.
>
> **Highest point**: Rawhead, near Bickerton in central Cheshire, rises 227 metres/746 feet above sea level.
>
> **Total ascent**: Total ascent/descent for the whole Trail is 1268 metres/4160 feet.
>
> **Dog friendliness**: Dogs are welcome but should be kept under close control, especially near farm buildings and livestock. Please consider other walkers and clean up after your dog.

Origins of the Trail

The Sandstone Trail was one of the earliest middle-distance ways in Britain, and the first true 'Cheshire Way'. Conceived by Cheshire County Council's Countryside and Recreation Department in the early 1970s, the Trail was officially opened in 1974. Its popularity has grown ever since, and today an estimated 150,000 walkers a year use paths along the route.

In the early days the Sandstone Trail was shorter than it is now, and stretched only 25 kilometres/16 miles between Delamere and Duckington, in central Cheshire. But the Trail was such an immediate success that it was soon lengthened to cover 50 kilometres/32 miles between Beacon Hill, above Frodsham, in the north, to Grindley Brook locks, on the Cheshire/Shropshire border, in the south. The Trail was extended yet again in the late 1990s to link Frodsham, on the Mersey, and Whitchurch, in Shropshire. This not only makes it easier to reach by public transport, but also allows walkers to enjoy the many excellent facilities of the towns at either end.

What is it like?

For most of the way, the Sandstone Trail sticks closely to Cheshire's central wooded sandstone ridge, often high above the Cheshire Plain. The numerous hill sections naturally include several steep ascents and descents with timber-edged and natural rock steps, occasional cliff edges and numerous open viewpoints. Where the Trail winds through Delamere Forest Park, the route follows surfaced forest tracks and paths. The central section of the Trail incorporates several attractive sections of ancient green lane. Where there are gaps in the hills, between Tarporley and Beeston and south of Larkton Hill towards the Cheshire-Shropshire border, the Trail crosses undulating Cheshire farmland punctuated with scattered farms and hamlets, streams, copses and scores of flooded marl pits. The southernmost section of the Trail follows the Llangollen arm of the Shropshire Union Canal between Willeymoor Lock and Whitchurch. For much of its route, the Trail deliberately traverses open countryside with few towns. Nonetheless, although the terrain along the Sandstone Trail is always interesting and varied, it is seldom challenging.

Marking the way *Bright yellow waymarkers featuring a black boot-print stamped with the letter 'S' make it easy to follow the Sandstone Trail*

Using the Trail

The Trail offers unbroken walking over some of the finest countryside in Cheshire. High ground has always been a magnet to walkers; and for most of the way the route follows the dramatic, wooded sandstone ridge that runs roughly from top to bottom across the Cheshire Plain. With its beautiful scenery and wide and ever-changing views, it's an invigorating walk at any time of year.

Please remember that the Trail is for walkers only; mountain bikes are actively discouraged, and horses are welcome only on short stretches of designated bridleway.

Most people choose to walk the Trail in sections to suit their individual style and pace. The route can be joined at countless places along the way, and the well managed and waymarked side paths give easy access to towns, villages, pubs, cafés and other amenities. They also provide a wealth of potential circular routes.

For twelve well-planned, and immensely popular circular walks along the Trail, see the companion book, *Circular Walks along the Sandstone Trail* by Carl Rogers (ISBN 978-1-902512-10-5). You may also like the new pocket-sized book in the popular Top 10 Walks series for *Cheshire: Easy Walks from the Sandstone Trail*, by Tony Bowerman (ISBN 978-1-908632-32-6).

Cheshire West and Chester County Council's website splits the Trail into three roughly equal parts. Each section is around 18 kilometres/11 miles: an enjoyable day's walk in one direction for anyone who is reasonably fit. Others choose to spread the journey across two days, staying overnight at a suitable

Sense of achievement *Tired but happy, a group of walkers approach the northern end of the Sandstone Trail*

halfway stop in Higher Burwardsley, close to Beeston Castle, or in Tarporley.

Alternatively, a few of the central inns, hotels and bed and breakfasts cater specifically for walkers and will transport you to the start of your day's walk in the morning and collect you again in the evening, just in time for a welcome hot bath and dinner. Ask individual accommodation providers for details.

Seasoned walkers can complete the Trail in one go; this is best achieved during the long summer days and takes around twelve hours. But be warned: it's a long way; as one weary walker remarked 'for the last few miles I was half asleep'.

More extreme still is the Sandstone Trail Race held in mid-autumn each year, when serious competitors attempt to run non-stop from Grindley Brook or Beeston Castle to Delamere Forest. The race draws competitors from a wide area, and has established some impressive records over the years.

Maps

The best maps for exploring the Sandstone Trail are those published by the Ordnance Survey. Although the Trail is shown on the silver and magenta covered Landranger 1:50,000 series, the larger scale, extra detail, and field boundaries of the orange covered Explorer 1:25,000 series make them every serious walker's map of choice. Two Explorer maps cover the Trail: 267 *Northwich and Delamere Forest* [North] and 257 *Crewe and Nantwich* [South]. Excerpts from these maps are used throughout this book. Better still, is the handy, pocket-size map book covering the whole Trail, *Walking Cheshire's Sandstone Trail: Large-scale, Enhanced Ordnance Survey Maps for the Sandstone Trail* (ISBN 978-1-908632-96-8).

Accommodation

There is plenty of accommodation either along or within easy walking distance to the Sandstone Trail. An updated list is prepared each year by Cheshire West and Chester Council's Countryside Management team and copies are distributed to relevant Tourist Information Centres (TICs). More than fifty places to stay are listed from north to south along the Trail, ranging from comfortable hotels and historic inns to friendly farmhouses and local bed and breakfast accommodation. Copies of the list can either be consulted at TICs or requested from them as a digital version sent via email. You can also download a PDF version of the accommodation list from the Sandstone Trail's own dedicated website: **www.sandstonetrail.co.uk**.

Connecting Routes

Several other middle- and long-distance routes connect with the Sandstone Trail. Most are shown and named on the Ordnance Survey Explorer series maps. These routes give walkers the option of continuing on across country, or creating their own long-distance circular walks.

The main routes linking to the Sandstone Trail include:

Northern Section:

Delamere Way	(Frodsham to Stockton Heath);
Eddisbury Way	(Frodsham to Higher Burwardsley);
North Cheshire Way	(Chester to Disley);
Weaver Valley Way	(Frodsham to Winsford);
Baker Way	Christleton to Delamere).

Central Section:

Eddisbury Way	(Burwardsley to Frodsham).

Southern Section:

Maelor Way	(Grindley Brook to Bron-y-Garth, on Offa's Dyke);
Marches Way	(Chester to Cardiff);
Shropshire Way	(Whitchurch spur of a circular route through Shrewsbury);
South Cheshire Way	(Grindley Brook to Mow Cop).

Making Sense of the
Sandstone Trail

The Unexpected Ridge

Most people think Cheshire is flat. But just how flat is that? Seen from the tops of the Clwydian Range to the west or the high moorland of the Peaks and Pennines to the east, Cheshire certainly seems as level and green as a pool table.

And yet… look carefully from those same Welsh or Derbyshire hills and in the middle distance you'll soon spot Cheshire's central sandstone ridge rising abruptly from the Plain. Suddenly, Cheshire is no longer really flat. Like an exclamation mark, the mid-Cheshire ridge lends unexpected verticality to an otherwise level landscape. And it's precisely that contrast that makes the ridge so dramatic.

What's more, Cheshire's backbone is the only high ground west of the Pennines and east of the Welsh hills. Like rocky vertebrae covered by a soft skin of trees, heather and gorse, the ridge's interlocking scarps sweep in a series of green arcs from north to south down the county, dividing it almost in half.

Triassic Sandstone

At the heart of this sandstone spine is isolated Beeston Crag, capped by the ruins of a medieval castle. Seen from afar, the crag's prominence must surely have acted like a magnet to our ancient ancestors. Today, farmland and wooded hills stretch away on either side. Across the Beeston Gap, the ridge runs north along the low-lying Delamere Ridge, through Delamere Forest, and on towards Frodsham and the Mersey estuary. To the south, the tree-clad sandstone ridge undulates past Peckforton Castle and Bulkeley Hill towards Rawhead and the Iron Age hillfort at Maiden Castle. Beyond that, on the Cheshire Plain, a vast ridge of gravel and sand deposited by the ice sheet during the last Ice Age stretches south towards Whitchurch and the Trail's end.

The mid-Cheshire ridge and its outliers are formed of layer upon layer of Triassic sandstones and pebble beds. These sedimentary rocks were laid down in semi-arid desert conditions, interspersed with occasional flash floods, between 225 and 195 million years ago. Dramatic sandstone cliffs and caves crop up all along the Trail. Today walkers can play their fingers over layers of rock formed over countless millennia by alternating wind-blown sand, rivers and floods.

Iron, Copper and Salt

These layers of sand and sediment were then consolidated over yet more millions of years by compression and mineral cementation. Minerals in solution were deposited around sand grains in the porous sandstone. Of these, the most common mineral was iron oxide (otherwise known as rust!). The minerals help cement the sand grains together. And the iron oxide gives the sandstone its striking, rich red and brown colouration.

Around the same time that the rock was being formed, evaporation of a warm, shallow sea or lagoon created the extensive underground salt deposits that lie beneath central Cheshire. Natural brine springs here have been exploited since at least the Iron Age. Dissolving salt beds beneath the southern end of the Trail also caused the spectacular 18th century collapse at Barhill Fall, on the modern Trail, near Tushingham.

Upheavals in the Earth's crust later vertically fractured or 'faulted' the horizontal sedimentary sandstones, which were then pushed upwards and tilted to create the modern ridge. Of course, these slow processes happened over unimaginable spans of time. Today the rock strata dip at a gentle angle

Cliffs and caves *Cheshire's 225-195 million year old Triassic sandstones are easily eroded into fissures, cliffs and caves*

Glacial pebbles *Around fifteen different types of ice-worn pebbles can be picked up along the Sandstone Trail*

of up to twelve degrees towards the east, with the contrasting crags of the steeper scarp slopes facing west across the broad Dee valley to the hazy outlines of the Clwydian hills.

More recently in geological terms, some time between 65 million and 1.6 million years ago, copper and other metals in solution were deposited from groundwater percolating along faults in the sandstone. Copper, in particular, was later mined from the sandstone hills both on Alderley Edge in east Cheshire and close to Bickerton on the Sandstone Trail.

Ice and Rock

These uplifted rocks were gradually eroded over the millennia, leaving the harder strata of the mid-Cheshire ridge protruding above the Plain. Then came the Ice Ages: a series of glaciations interspersed with warmer periods. During the most recent Ice Age, between 75,000 and 10,000 years ago, a vast ice sheet pushed in from the Irish Sea basin, depressing the surface of the earth and tearing away rock from the front of Helsby and Frodsham hills. The exact depth of the ice sheet can only be guessed at but it certainly overrode the mid-Cheshire ridge. In its stately progress down from the north and northwest, the ice sheet carried debris and rocks from southwest Scotland, northeast Ireland and the Lake District. At its maximum extent, the ice stretched just south of the modern Cheshire border, towards Wolverhampton, in the Midlands.

But when the climate eventually started to warm up towards the end of the Ice Age, between 20,000 and 10,000 years ago, the ice front gradually 'retreated'. As the ice receded, it dropped a thick layer of *boulder clay* or *glacial till* across much of Cheshire. The limey clays represent shell-rich deposits dredged from what had once been the floor of the Irish Sea. Only the mid-Cheshire ridge remained largely uncovered by *glacial till*—leaving exposed the older, distinctive Triassic sandstone rocks that we see today.

The ancient ice sheet also scattered 'foreign' boulders and pebbles across Cheshire. Known as *glacial erratics*, these typically granite or volcanic rocks are readily distinguished from the local red sandstone. Look for large, greyish, ice-rounded boulders built into walls or cleared to field edges along the Trail. Some display long, parallel scratches made by debris held in the ice. You can also pick up fifteen or so different kinds of smooth, ice-worn glacial pebbles, dropped by the ice sheet, from paths and tracks along the Trail.

There's a wealth of other interesting late-glacial and post-glacial features to look out for along the Trail, too. At Urchin's Kitchen and the delightfully-named Dog Fall, near Willington, walkers can enter deep glacial drainage channels scoured out under immense pressure beneath the ice sheet. Near Utkinton the Trail skirts a whaleback-shaped hill of sand deposited by the ice, called a *drumlin*. Between Duckington—at the southern end of the sandstone ridge—and Whitchurch, the Trail runs along the top of a vast bank of sand and rock, or *terminal moraine*, dumped by the ice front as it paused during its final 'retreat'.

Meltwater, Meres and Marshes

By the time the ice was gone from Cheshire, around 18,000 to 16,000 years ago, the landscape had been reshaped. From time to time, great meltwater lakes flooded parts of the Cheshire Plain. Elsewhere, the surging waters of overflow channels gouged through the sandstone ridge, reshaping the Mouldsworth Gap, Organsdale and the Beeston Gap. At the southern end of the Trail, both Grindley Brook and the Llangollen Canal follow a broad glacial drainage channel cut through the Duckington-Whitchurch *terminal moraine*.

Where the sediment-laden water spilled into further lakes, fans of sand and gravel settled on the bottom. These naturally graded deposits are quarried today, particularly east of Delamere Forest and southeast of the Beeston Gap. There are flooded sandpits just south of Larkton Hall; and even the Barnsbridge Gates car park in Delamere Forest is an old gravel pit.

As time passed, most of the meltwater lakes dried out, leaving numerous wet, peaty hollows or *mosses*. Cheshire mosses were common even in the recent past; but most have since been drained and ploughed for agriculture. Good examples along the Trail include Fullers Moor, near Bickerton, and Willeymoor, east of the *terminal moraine* at Tushingham. A few glacial meres survive, too. Once drained for forestry, Blakemere, in Delamere Forest, has recently been allowed to reflood. In contrast, Peckforton Mere, east of the Trail below the Peckforton Hills, is a surviving glacial pool, now filled by the infant River Gowy.

Hunter-Gatherers

The period following the end of the last Ice Age is known as the Mesolithic or Middle Stone Age. Lowland Cheshire remained wet: a sodden morass of marshes, mosses and meres interspersed with birch forest. By around 8,000BC, early hunter-gatherers were moving through the trees, fishing, trapping game and collecting roots, nuts and berries. Scatters of their delicate flint weapons and tools, or microliths, have been found across Cheshire. Evidence of Mesolithic tool making in Cheshire has been uncovered, for example, in a cave at Carden Park, not far from the Sandstone Trail.

When the practice of farming arrived in Britain from mainland Europe around 4,000BC, it marked the beginning of the Neolithic or New Stone Age. Rearing primitive sheep and cattle and cultivating early varieties of wheat and barley offered a more reliable source of food than hunting and gathering. Neolithic farmers cut clearings in the forest and established the first permanent settlements. They developed new stone tools to match their new lifestyle: stone hammers, flint knives and chisels, flint scrapers for cleaning skins, and polished stone axes for chopping down trees.

Along the Ridgeway

Polished stone axes, gold and salt were traded over huge distances. A network of long distance tracks grew up across Britain, hugging the drier and more open high ground. Keeping to the ridges was simpler and safer than pushing through the marshy lowland forests. On the modern Sandstone Trail, walkers are following in the footsteps of Neolithic traders moving along an ancient ridgeway between the Mersey and the Severn. So it's no surprise that Neolithic stone tools crop up all along the ridge. Typical finds include: 'five wedge-shaped polished stone axes at the foot of Eddisbury Hill, 1895', and 'a flint arrowhead found on a stretch of the Sandstone Trail between Beeston and Peckforton Castles'.

Metal tools were first worked in Britain at the start of the Bronze Age, around 2,500BC. As the population grew, permanent farmsteads spread across Cheshire. Like their Neolithic ancestors, Bronze Age farmers favoured the lighter, easier to cultivate soils along the ridge. Evidence of Bronze Age settlement has been found at Eddisbury hillfort and on Beeston Crag. Bronze Age tribes buried their important dead beneath circular mounds called barrows or *lows*; several clusters of these also occur along the ridge, including a group at Seven Lows Farm, near Delamere. Bronze Age axes, too, have often been found close to the ridge, particularly around Beeston.

Clearing the trees *Stone axe hammers like this painstakingly hand polished example found near the Sandstone Trail at Beeston, were an essential part of every Neolithic farmer's tool kit*

But probably the most exciting finds in Cheshire from this period are a solid gold torc, or necklace, and a pair of twisted gold armlets uncovered by workmen near Hampton Heath, close to the southern end of the Trail, in 1831. These stunning ancient status symbols can now be admired in the Manchester Museum.

As the climate got wetter and colder during the late Bronze Age/early Iron Age, defended settlements called hillforts sprang up along the sandstone ridge. Population growth combined with the spread of new iron weapons made it a dangerous time to be alive. Earthworks topped with wooden palisades surrounded groups of thatched round houses, storage huts and animal pens. Hillforts along the mid-Cheshire ridge include those at Woodhouse Hill, Eddisbury, Kelsborrow, Beeston, and Maiden Castle. Other defended settlements occur nearby on Helsby Hill, at Bradley above the River Weaver at Frodsham, and on the banks of Oakmere, near Delamere.

Romans and Anglo-Saxons

Life changed again with the Roman invasion of AD43. The powerful new legionary fortress of *Deva* was completed at Chester around AD79. A network of new roads linked it to other local settlements including the trading port at Meols on the tip of the Wirral, the industrial settlement at Wilderspool, near Warrington, and the ancient brine springs of central Cheshire. Cheshire's best-known Roman road, Watling Street, ran between *Deva* (Chester) and *Mamucium* (Manchester). It crossed the central ridge immediately below Eddisbury Hillfort, where a section of the road can still be traced through Nettleford Wood and nearby Organsdale field today. The sole Roman villa discovered so far in Cheshire is at Eaton-by-Tarporley, just to the east of the Trail; though it's said that crop marks seen on aerial photographs close to Beeston Castle may indicate another. Further south on the Trail, a rare Roman bronze military diploma was found by ditchers in a field near No Man's Heath, in 1812.

When the Romans finally abandoned their province of *Britannia* in AD410, land-hungry Angles and Saxons from northern Germany and Scandinavia swept in to colonise much of eastern Britain. Cheshire remained a frontier zone until the end of the 7th century, when it was annexed by the Anglo-Saxon kingdom of Mercia. These first English settlers cleared woodland on the Cheshire Plain and built settlements along the spring line below the sandstone ridge. Anglo-Saxon place names can be recognised by the suffixes *leah* or *ley*, meaning a glade or clearing in the forest, *ham*, meaning homestead or village, and *tun*, meaning farm. Saxon clearings around Delamere, for example, include: Kingsley—the 'king's clearing'; Norley—or 'north clearing'; and Manley—or the 'common wood clearing'. Further south are Tarporley, Burwardsley, and Bulkeley. Similarly, Saxon settlements along the Trail include: Frodsham, Overton, Willington, Utkinton, Beeston, Peckforton, Bickerton, Larkton, Hampton and Tushingham.

Viking attacks from the sea began in the late 8th century. To protect themselves, the Saxons constructed a line of fortified *burghs* between Chester and Manchester. As part of these defences, King Alfred's daughter Aethelflaeda hurriedly rebuilt the long abandoned Iron Age hillfort at Eddisbury, on the sandstone ridge. The Danes were held back and a succession of Saxon earls governed Cheshire as part of the Anglo-Saxon kingdom of Mercia until the Norman Conquest of 1066.

Norman Cheshire

The Norman Conquest marked another watershed in English history. Chester was one of the last Saxon/English rebel strongholds. But in the winter of 1069-70 the area was 'laid waste' by the Norman army, and their commander, Hugh Lupus 'the wolf' became Cheshire's first Norman earl.

Under the Norman feudal system the king gave land to his lords, who in turn allocated manorial land to their own supporters. Fertile Saxon farmland in southwest Cheshire, between the River Dee and the central sandstone ridge, was carved up into large estates.

Many of these Norman estates still exist today. In fact, a large, almost continuous block of ancient estates survives south of Chester. They include the Eaton, Peckforton, Carden, Bolesworth, Cholmondeley and Arderne estates. No wonder John Speed, the famous eighteenth century mapmaker who was born at Farndon, called Cheshire the '*seede plot of gentility*'. Even today, Cheshire is still in many ways a feudal county. For almost a thousand years, these Cheshire estates—which stretch from immediately south of Chester almost down to the Shropshire border—have acted as a buffer against industry and development. Today, the Sandstone Trail runs through many of these large, abutting private landholdings, which are still characterised by scattered villages, comparatively sparse population and unspoilt countryside. They remain a valuable sanctuary for wildlife.

Hunting and Horses

Cheshire's Norman rulers loved hunting and appropriated vast tracts of woodland and 'waste' for their sport. 'Forest' didn't mean woodland in the way it does today, but rather any land set aside for the chase. Another 'chase' existed on the Peckforton hills in the 1340s. These jealously guarded hunting preserves affected settlement patterns and agriculture across much of north Cheshire for centuries. Today, Delamere Forest Park is all that remains of the once huge 'forests' of *Mara* and *Mondrem*.

Cheshire's longstanding love of horses and hunting arguably dates back a thousand years or so to Norman times. Chester Races are the oldest flat

Castle of the rock *High on its isolated sandstone crag, medieval Beeston Castle promises visitors some of the most dramatic panoramic views in England*

races in the country. The Tarporley Hunt was established in 1762 and is one of the oldest in the country, and Cheshire remains a keen hunting county; Tarporley Races were a fashionable social event from 1775 until 1938 (the old racecourse lies alongside the Trail just north of Tarporley); and today those same ancient equestrian skills are celebrated on the Cheshire polo grounds.

But the most outstanding relic of Cheshire's Norman past is undoubtedly Beeston Castle on its isolated crag at the heart of the sandstone ridge. Built in the 1220s by Earl Ranulph III, the castle incorporates Saracen features picked up during his time at the Crusades. Within the inner bailey is the deepest historic well in England, said to conceal Richard II's 'lost treasure'. The castle was later besieged during the Civil War.

Townfields and Halls

As the Middle Ages progressed, more of Cheshire was cleared for cultivation. Land was worked communally in open arable fields and common meadows. Evidence survives in field-names such as 'Townfield' or 'Everyman's Field'; 'Townfields' still exist close to the Trail at Frodsham and Tiverton, for example. The soil was ploughed into raised beds and a different person farmed each strip. Where modern ploughing hasn't obliterated them, these undulating, gently 'S' shaped 'swing plough patterns', or 'ridge and furrow' marks can still be seen; good examples along the Trail survive in fields just south of Oxpasture Wood and north of Crib Lane, near Tarporley; others can be seen near Iddenshall Rough, near Tarporley, and in pastureland on the slopes below St. Chad's chapel at Tushingham.

Each manor had its own manor house or hall. These 'family seats' are a defining feature of Cheshire. Usually built outside the villages, the halls were often 'black-and-white' timber-framed buildings. Notable examples along the Trail, from north to south, include: Austerson Old Hall, relocated near Alvanley; Utkinton Hall; Hulgrave Hall and Tiverton Hall near Tiverton; Broxton Old Hall below Bickerton; Hampton Old Hall and Tushingham Hall.

Manor houses and monastic granges were often protected by a moat, and in many cases the moat is all that remains. Over 200 moated sites are known across Cheshire. One of the largest and best survives at Iddenshall Rough, a few hundred metres west of the Trail, near Tarporley. Another well-preserved possible moat can be seen beside the Trail to the east of Manor House Farm, near Hampton Heath.

Saltways and Turnpikes

Cheshire's already ancient salt industry prospered during the Middle Ages. Saltwater from natural brine springs was evaporated in lead pans at the traditional salt producing towns of Northwich, Nantwich and Middlewich. The dry salt was then packed into sacks and baskets. Trains of plodding packhorses carried Cheshire salt into Lancashire, Derbyshire and Wales along ancient saltways radiating out from the salt towns. Many of the saltways heading for either the Port of Chester or Wales cross the Sandstone Trail at gaps in the hills. Place names incorporating the word 'salt' include 'Salterswell' at Tarporley and 'Salters Bridge', near Tarvin. Major saltways crossing the Trail include the old Roman Watling Street, below Eddisbury hillfort; the Nantwich to Tarvin road via Tarporley; and the Nantwich to North Wales saltersway (now the A534) that crosses the hills at Gallantry Bank, near Bickerton, on its way to the medieval bridge over the Dee at Farndon. Lesser packhorse routes traversed the hills at Higher Burwardsley and through the Peckforton Gap. Local farmers, itinerant preachers and pedlars continued to use these same routes for centuries.

For several miles between Bickerton Hill and Hampton Post, the Sandstone Trail runs parallel to the old Chester-to-London coach road. As traffic grew from the late 1600s onwards, the roads deteriorated and were often impassable in winter. People and horses were said to have drowned in the potholes. The old system in which local parishes were responsible for the roads within their boundaries became increasingly unfair. So private turnpike trusts were set up by Acts of Parliament to construct and maintain new toll roads. Toll bars were set up at Grindley Brook near Whitchurch in 1759, and at Gresty's Waste near Kelsall in 1769—where the old tollkeeper's cottage survives today beside the Trail.

Canals, Railways and Footpaths

Britain's canal era started at roughly the same time. The canals' primary role was to carry heavy raw materials such as marl, lime and fuel for the expanding agricultural industry. The Chester to Nantwich stretch of what is now the Shropshire Union Canal below Beeston Castle was completed in 1779. But to the canal company's surprise and chagrin, the newfangled railways arrived hot on their heels. When the Crewe to Holyhead line through the Beeston Gap opened for business in 1836, it soon pushed the company who owned the adjacent canal into bankruptcy. A year later, the penniless canal company sold its lease to the railway. Canal traffic today is entirely recreational.

Outside the main arterial routes however, life continued much as always. For Cheshire villagers, the turnpikes, canals and railways were largely irrelevant. People walked to work, school, church or chapel as they always had, creating the maze of footpaths that criss-cross the ridge. Central Cheshire's network of narrow lanes, too, remained as unsurfaced tracks until the 1930s and beyond. Along them travelled smallholders from the hills riding to the weekly markets in Chester or Whitchurch, the postman with his bugle to call people to collect their letters, and the huckster, or horse-drawn 'taxi driver', in his high cart or chandry. Our quiet country lanes changed markedly only with the spread of the motorcar.

Settlement along the Sandstone Trail

Settlement patterns along the Sandstone Trail vary enormously and are affected by three main factors: Delamere's ancient forest law, the underlying soils, and the water supply.

During the Middle Ages, roughly two-fifths of modern Cheshire was covered by the three vast hunting forests of Wirral, Delamere, and Macclesfield. Delamere Forest was itself made up of two smaller ancient forests called *Mara* and *Mondrem*. Together, they covered most of the land bordered by the Mersey estuary and the rivers Gowy and Weaver.

For over 700 years, from the Norman Conquest until the early 1800s, forest law meant that a huge area around modern Delamere Forest was out of bounds to any meaningful large-scale farming, settlement or other development. Hundreds of people still lived in the forest, of course, but their rights were severely curtailed. Only a few small areas were legally 'disafforested'—such as the manors of Weaverham, Over, and Tarvin. Otherwise, forest law meant there were few farms, and even fewer settlements or churches, across much of northern Cheshire.

Soil, Squatters and Smallholders

As you might expect, the underlying rocks and soils also affect where people settle. Soils along the Sandstone Trail include glacial sands, gravels and clays, with peat in several once boggy areas. These in turn affect agriculture, and the Trail runs through several distinct farming areas, each determined by what does best on the local soil.

Surprisingly perhaps, opinion over exactly what constitutes the 'best' soil has changed over the centuries. Back in prehistoric times, the mid-Cheshire ridge was the place to be. High and dry above the lowland meres, mosses and tangled woodlands, the ridge promised security, a place on the strategic trade route that ran along the ridgeway—and light, easy to work, sandy soils.

But as settlements spread across the newly cleared, heavier but more fertile lowland soils from the Saxon period onwards, the ridge seemed progressively less attractive. Sandy soil now seemed a poor second best. Our Cheshire ancestors moved down to the lowlands, and the hills were eventually abandoned to smallholders, squatters and open heathland.

Yet ironically, in recent years the trend has come full circle. For very different and more modern reasons, those same ridge top smallholdings and sandstone cottages have now become the sought after rural retreats of Cheshire's prosperous few. For them, the soil is of little importance. Once more, Cheshire folk dream of a place in the hills.

But for farms and farmers, soil remains king. The northern section of the Trail, extending from Alvanley through Delamere to Utkinton is characterised by light, sandy loams ideal for early 'Cheshires', maincrop potatoes and fruit. Commercial fruit farms and a plant nursery thrive above the frost line on the southwest facing slopes between Kelsall and Willington. The poorest and sandiest glacial soils to the east of the Kelsall Ridge are reserved for modern Delamere Forest's coniferous plantations.

As the soils become heavier south of Willington so the farming changes to mixed dairy and arable. From Utkinton to Tiverton, the low-lying heavy loams and clays of the Beeston Gap were once permanent pastures that supported Cheshire's traditional dairy herds. Today the future of conventional farming is uncertain.

Moving further south—past Beeston Castle—the poor, thin soil on the sandstone ridge between Peckforton and Bickerton was traditionally left either as open heathland grazed by scattered cattle and sheep, or planted up with broadleaved trees. Only in a few places was the land reclaimed for farming by the application of copious muck, marl, lime and artificial fertilisers. Few modern walkers realise, perhaps, that the sandstone ridge's green mantle of trees is relatively new; until the 1930s and '40s, as old photographs show, the hills were bare.

Beyond the southern end of the sandstone hills, the Trail descends into open country. From Bickerton towards Whitchurch, the rolling glacial landscape contains a mosaic of underlying loams, sand and clays. These support a wider range of farming: both arable and fodder crops, and dairy cattle. Within living memory, much of the milk from Cheshire's dairy herds was made into cheese. Cheshire's flower-rich permanent pastures were believed to make the finest cheese; and early farm leases often prohibited ploughing without the landlord's consent. This quiet southwest corner of the county was once the stronghold of farmhouse Cheshire cheese.

Some say cheese was first made in Cheshire by the Romans and exported to feed their legions across the Empire. Certainly, Cheshire cheese has been famous since at least the Middle Ages; and by the 1700s thousands of tons were exported each year to London and elsewhere. Every farm had its cheese press and the cheese factor, or wholesaler, was an important man. There were still around 200 cheese-making farms in Cheshire in 1938, most of them on the rich, clay grasslands of southwest Cheshire. At one time there were regular cheese fairs at Whitchurch, Nantwich and Chester. Today, the Nantwich International Cheese Show (part of the Nantwich and South

Forest rides *A horse and trap pause on the grassy verge of the 'Switchback' road through Delamere Forest, in the 1920s*

Cheshire Show, held every July) is the largest cheese show in Europe. Sadly, only a handful of Cheshire farms make cheese today. One of the few still creating traditional, award winning farmhouse cheese is Larkton Hall Farm, on the Trail just south of Bickerton.

Marl Pits, Springs and Wells

Long before the use of lime and modern artificial fertilisers, Cheshire's poorer soils were often improved with a natural fertiliser called marl. 'Marling' is an ancient technique first practised by the Celts. It's a laborious process that involves digging out and spreading the naturally occurring lime-rich subsoils, or marls, that underlie much of Cheshire. The marls were originally carried here by a vast ice sheet during the last Ice Age. Their calcareous nature is due to the crushed shells they contain, scoured from the ancient sea floor. As a reminder of this now obsolete practice, several fields on the Trail at Utkinton, for example, retain old names like 'Marl Wood' or 'Big Marled Wood'.

Well deep *Beeston Castle's crag-top medieval well is the deepest historic well in England*

It's an arcane fact that Cheshire has more ponds than any other county in England—as a quick look at the larger scale Ordnance Survey maps will suggest. The majority are flooded marl pits, dug out originally by gangs of wandering contractors. Marl pits can be recognised by their regular shape, with three steep sides complemented by a shallower access ramp. Marl pits are especially common along the Trail on the low-lying, heavier soils between Utkinton and Beeston. Surviving marl pits provide valuable habitat for fish, frogs and newts, as well as water birds such as moorhens, coots and herons.

The third key factor affecting settlement patterns along the Trail is the water supply. The ridge's aptly named Waterstones are porous and act like a giant sponge, storing up and then releasing water at a steady rate. Two Cheshire rivers, the Weaver and the tiny Gowy, begin within a stone's throw of each other on the Peckforton Hills. Natural springs occur both at the foot of the hills and, occasionally, higher up on the ridge. Wells cut into the soft sandstone are plentiful too. Such a ready water supply meant people could settle virtually anywhere they liked and so farms along the Trail tend to be dispersed. Until piped water arrived just fifty or so years ago, every cottage and farm relied on their local spring or well for both themselves and their livestock. In times of drought, new wells were dug by local 'pump well sinkers'; alternatively, poorer cottagers could buy water by the bucket from the local water carrier.

Important springs along the Trail included Swan's Well at Manley Common, Pearl Hole at Willington, Beeston Spring below Beeston Castle, Droppingstone Well at Bickerton, and that at Pearl Farm, Tushingham. A search of old maps shows many more. A few so-called mineral springs along the ridge were also widely credited with health-giving powers: in particular Whistlebitch Well in Primrosehill Wood, and Horsley Bath below Peckforton Castle. Finally, a document of 1620 mentions a 'holy well' close to Old Saint Chad's chapel, at Tushingham.

Many of these ancient springs and wells are dry today, their water usurped by a line of pumping stations at the base of the Bickerton hills owned by the Staffordshire Water Board. Water is extracted elsewhere along the ridge for farms, a bottling plant and a brewery. Over the last few decades the Cheshire water table has fallen dramatically and even the deep, historic, crag-top well at Beeston Castle is dry.

Quarries and Caves

On a still drier note, the ridge's softer sandstones have often either been naturally eroded or deliberately dug out to form caves. The best natural cave (although clearly enhanced by man) on the Trail is probably Mad Allen's Hole near Bickerton; another is Musket's Hole, south of Rawhead. Other, man-made, caves include what may be underground Civil War stables within the grounds of Beeston Castle (now blocked off to protect bats, and for public safety), and the spectacular Queen's Parlour, and smaller Bloody Bones Cave beneath Rawhead—both of which were excavated originally for their soft white scouring sand.

Finally, there are undoubtedly ancient shafts and tunnels radiating out into the darkness deep beneath the sandstone ridge close to the copper mine chimney at Gallantry Bank. There's even a hidden adit, or gently sloping tunnel, that enters the hillside from a shallow hollow in the woods beside the Trail.

The sandstone ridge has been deliberately quarried, too, for building stone since at least the Middle Ages. But Cheshire's sandstone is far from uniform. In fact, the quality varies hugely depending on the grain size and degree of mineral cementation. The finest hard, pale building stone from quarries at Manley Knoll was used at Chester Castle and Eaton Hall, while stone from King's Chair in Delamere Forest was reputedly carted away along the old Roman road to build Vale Royal Abbey near Whitegate, in central Cheshire. Beeston Castle was built with stone cut from its own hill top moat, while nearby Victorian Peckforton Castle was constructed with sandstone dug from a dedicated ridge top quarry, now lost amid trees on the Peckforton Hills.

Smaller local quarries along the ridge provided hand cut stone for homes, farms and outbuildings. All are now abandoned, but interesting quarries along the Trail can be seen at Overton Hill, Alvanley Cliff, Manley Knoll, Hangingstone Hill, Utkinton, above Fisher's Green, Ash Hill near Tarporley, high on Stanner Nab at Peckforton, below Rawhead Farm, and near Maiden Castle. Especially on the Peckforton and Bickerton hills, look out, too, for cottages, farms and walls built with large, hand-cut sandstone blocks.

Building Materials

Cheshire's vernacular architecture crops up all along the Trail. Keep an eye out, in particular, for our distinctive 'black and white' half-timbered cottages

Bat cave *Now barred off to protect roosting bats, this deep cave within the grounds of Beeston Castle may once have been used as stables during the English Civil War*

and solid, sandstone-block built homes and farms. Some of the older farmhouses have grand Georgian frontages, too, added at a time when Cheshire agriculture was in its prime.

The earliest 'black and white' buildings feature curved timber 'A' frame, or 'cruck', end gables. The whole timber box frame sits on a low sandstone foundation wall to keep it dry above the damp ground. Such houses would originally have been thatched but most now have more recent slate roofs and brick chimneys. Similarly, the original whitewashed 'wattle and daub' walls of mixed clay and cow dung plastered over woven hazel have long since been replaced by brick infill, or 'noggin'. Still others have been wholly plastered over, and little outward trace of their timber frames survives. In most cases, the old wooden mullion windows, too, have been replaced by iron casements.

Outstanding half-timbered houses and pubs on the northern section of the Trail include: the 'Ring o' Bells pub at Overton; Austerson Old Hall below Alvanley Cliff; the 'cruck' framed old smithy, in Beeston village; Moathouse Farm, on Horsley Lane; and a cottage above Pennsylvania Wood. The much altered Pheasant Inn at Higher Burwardsley still features both original half-timbering and block-built sandstone outbuildings; while a tiny, well-preserved sandstone and 'cruck' framed cottage survives below Peckforton Gap. To the south is Manor House Farm, near Hampton; brick infilled Pearl Farm, and the unspoilt Blue Bell Inn at Bell o' th' Hill, near Tushingham.

Equally, notable buildings along the Trail constructed of large, hand-cut blocks of sandstone include: The Bear's Paw, Frodsham; New Pale Lodge, Manley; Eddisbury Lodge, Delamere; Roughlow Farm and Rock Farm, at Willington; Fishersgreen Farm, near Tarporley; Castlegate Farm, Beeston; cottages at Higher Burwardsley; Peckforton Gap Lodge; Chiflik Farm, near Gallantry Bank; and Larkton Hall, south of the Bickerton Hills.

Within Living Memory

As the Sandstone Trail grows more popular with each passing year, we should pause to remember how much quieter central Cheshire was even in the recent past. Society was more stratified but less mobile, and everyone knew everyone else's business. Cheshire's jigsaw of large estates held real sway over the people who lived on them and worked for them. It's also said there was, and still is, a deep and ancient rivalry—stretching back to Agincourt and beyond—between some of the established Cheshire families who own those estates.

There was friendly rivalry, too, between the ordinary people who lived on either side of the hills. Cheshire's central sandstone ridge acted as a watershed in more ways than one. While the farmers and smallholders on the western flanks of the hills travelled to market in Chester, those on the eastern side gravitated towards the markets at Nantwich and Whitchurch. Places separated by a few miles may as well have been continents apart.

Where the Trail brings walkers and visitors today, there was once only rural isolation characterised by occasional movements and relative silence.

How things change.

Walking the Sandstone Trail

Section 1: Frodsham to Manley Common

Distance:	5½ miles/9 kilometres
Duration:	Allow 2-3 hours
Difficulty:	Moderate: Some steep ascents and descents
Parking:	Frodsham
Refreshments:	Pubs and cafés in Frodsham; Ring o' Bells opposite Overton Church, Frodsham; Manley Farm Shop, Manley; Goshawk, Mouldsworth

Outline: *Along the wooded sandstone ridge: steep ascent, estuary views, clifftop paths, sandstone staircase, Iron Age hillfort, wildflower meadow, open woodland, nature reserves, old hall, green lanes and common land.*

MAP A A sculptured sandstone and steel obelisk outside the Bear's Paw on **Main Street**, Frodsham marks the northern starting point for Cheshire's Sandstone Trail. Cross the road and walk up Church Street, beneath the railway bridge. Continue uphill, past Eddisbury Square, Kingsway and Churchfield Road on your right. Less than 50 metres beyond Churchfield Road, turn right, up steps, onto a signposted footpath that rises between gardens to **Overton Church** **1**.

▲ *Helsby Hill from Woodhouse Hill*

Section one: *Frodsham to Manley Common* 37

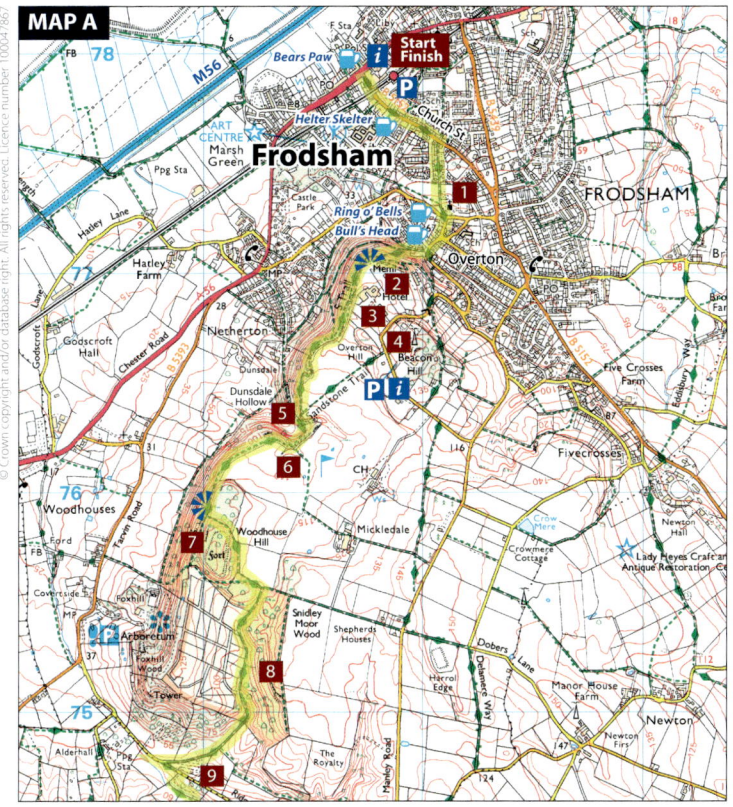

Cross Howey Lane and walk up Bellemonte Road alongside the black-and-white 'Ring o' Bells' pub. When the road bends left, beyond the Bull's Head, turn right, up Middle Walk. A hundred metres on, at the foot of the densely wooded slopes of Overton Hill, bear left on a sandy path amid the trees. Almost immediately, turn left again, uphill on a steep, signposted path. The path zigzags up through mature woodland: turn sharp left at a waymarked junction, then sharp right at the next T-junction onto a level path along the contour of the slope. Close to the top, turn left, up the bank, on another waymarked path, to emerge into the light and breeze near the **War Memorial** **2**.

The view is stunning. Dominated by the sky, the panorama spans the vast, watery expanse of the Mersey Estuary with Liverpool's distinctive skyline forming a dramatic backdrop. In the middle distance, beyond the M56, are the vast dredging lagoons of the Manchester Ship Canal, and the open expanse of the old Frodsham Marshes, now reclaimed for agriculture, a wind farm and industry.

Beyond the memorial, the waymarked Trail runs on along the edge, where a metal sign warns: 'Danger, unfenced cliffs'. When the path forks at a line of low sandstone cliffs, take the righthand, lower path that runs along their base. The next section of the path towards Dunsdale Hollow has been popular for well over a century and was once known as the 'Ladies' Path'; look out for 100- to 150-year-old graffiti carved into the sandstone cliffs. Up to the left is **Overton Hill** **3**, site of the old Mersey View Pleasure Grounds and funfair.

The path winds through open oak and birch woodland, bright with bluebells in the spring. Beyond an old spoon-shaped quarry, the Trail drops downslope to a signposted T-junction. Off to the left is the **Beacon Hill** **4** car park, an alternative—and at one time, the original—starting point for the Trail. Instead, turn right, to follow the path carefully around the top of unfenced sandstone cliffs. Crude steps cut into the rock here once descended into the shaded combe of Dunsdale Hollow. Known locally as **Jacob's Ladder** **5**, the steps are now dangerously eroded; today, safer metal steps—Baker's Dozen—descend the cliffs ahead.

From a signposted junction towards the bottom of the hollow, take the broad, lefthand path that rises up the far side. Beyond a wooden footbridge, go up another set of steps cut into a low sandstone cliff—known as **Abraham's Leap** **6**. At the top, bear right and follow the winding path through trees with the greens and fairways of Frodsham Golf Course on your left. Beyond the golf course, the Trail continues to an open rock platform, called Scout Rock, at Woodhouse Viewpoint, with broad vistas across the fields to Helsby Crag.

Bear left, away from the edge, on a rising path over Woodhouse Hill. Lost among the trees and bracken on the high ground to the right here are the Iron Age earthworks of **Woodhouse Hillfort** **7**. As the path drops downhill again, with fields ahead, bear right on a waymarked path skirting the edge of the woods. Soon, the path curves to the left, to arrive at a signposted

T-junction at the start of **Snidley Moor Wood** 8 which, like Woodhouse Hill, is owned and managed by the Woodland Trust. Turn right, away from the fields, downhill on the gently sloping, sandy byway beneath the trees. Off to the right, a series of former pig grazing fields have been replanted with native woodland species. Lower down, the path narrows and becomes an atmospheric sunken lane with high, overgrown banks on either side.

After the Trail leaves the woods, the track becomes sandy and curves beside a large pond. Continue past a static home site, to meet the narrow country road known as the Ridgeway.

Nature Notes

The view from Frodsham hill was different in the past. Tidal marshes and reedbeds reached far inland until at least the Middle Ages. But when the Manchester Ship Canal's 'Big Ditch' cut off the marshland from the sea in 1894, much of this wildlife-rich wilderness was reclaimed for farmland and industry. Countless skeins of noisy geese passed overhead at dawn and dusk until Stanlow refinery was built in 1922. Even so, the Mersey and Frodsham Marshes and the vast dredging lagoons of the Manchester Ship Canal still support a multitude of birds, including an impressive list of rare waders and birds of prey.

Ancient **Overton Church** 1 stands on high ground overlooking the Mersey. It was heavily restored and rebuilt in 1880-3 and, from the outside at least, appears Victorian. However, Saint Laurence's contains many Norman features and occupies the site of an earlier Saxon church mentioned in the Domesday Book. The base of an ancient cross surmounted by an eighteenth century sundial survives in the churchyard.

Overton Hill with helter-skelter, Jubilee Day, 1937

Several local landowners donated land to Frodsham Parish Council in the 1920s as a site for the **War Memorial** 2, which commemorates local men who died in the 'Great War' of 1914-18. The sandstone obelisk was built by Palmers Stone Masons. The surrounding open space is held in trust for the enjoyment of Frodsham people forever.

The Mersey View Pavilion and Pleasure Grounds on the summit of **Overton Hill** 3 was built by the Parker-Hoose family and opened in 1865. On weekends and holidays, local people let their hair down on the American swingboats, donkey rides and ball games, drank tea or beer, and danced on the 'Green'. The popular helter-skelter was added in 1908 at a cost of £300.

Perhaps as early as the 13th century, **Beacon Hill** 4 was the site of one of a chain of huge signal bonfires, or beacons, used to warn the country of imminent danger or invasion. Lookouts watched for

The 'Ladies Path', on a treeless Overton Hill, around 1900

fires on Halton Castle, Bidston Hill, Alderley Edge and Mow Cop before lighting their own. Today, Beacon Hill hosts the beacon's modern equivalent: a series of microwave communication masts.

During the early 1900s, a popular promenade called the 'Ladies' Path' traversed the steep sides of Overton Hill. A flight of steps called **Jacob's Ladder** 5 —after the biblical 'stairway to heaven'—was cut into the cliffs for the precarious descent into Dunsdale Hollow. Now dangerously eroded, the rock steps have since been replaced by a metal flight called 'Baker's Dozen' in celebration of Jack Baker, one of the creators of the Sandstone Trail.

On the far side of Dunsdale Hollow (whose name actually means 'dung valley') is another, shorter flight of steps cut into the rock, called **Abraham's Leap** 6. When it was named, more than a century ago, almost everyone in a still predominantly churchgoing society would have recognised Abraham as Jacob's grandfather and one of the biblical founders of the twelve tribes of Israel.

Two Edwardian girls playing on Jacob's Ladder, Dunsdale, around 1910

Woodhouse Hillfort 7 is the northernmost of seven late Bronze/early Iron Age defended settlements on or near Cheshire's central sandstone ridge. It probably guarded a prehistoric ridgeway used by traders moving between the Mersey and the Severn. Excavations in 1951 showed the single earthen rampart was originally four metres wide and faced with drystone walling. Sandstone slingstones, flint arrowheads and a flint scraper have been found nearby.

The Woodland Trust cares for three areas on the Frodsham escarpment: Frodsham Hill Wood, Woodhouse Hill Wood, and **Snidley Moor Wood** 8. Together, they form part of the second largest continuous block of broadleaved woodland in Cheshire. Invasive bracken and non-native rhododendrons are rigorously controlled as part of the Trust's plan to ensure a gradual transition from mixed birch scrub to mature lowland oak woodland.

MAP B Turn sharp left, uphill, on the quiet, leafy lane called the Ridgeway. It's signposted for 'Delamere Forest' and 'Beeston Castle'. Less than 100 metres later, opposite the entrance to the 'Ridgeway Country Holiday Park', turn right, up a flight of stone steps and climb the bank into **Ridgeway Wood** **9**. Crude steps drop downhill through open, mature oak woodland. At the bottom of the slope, bear left, along the inside of the wood, keeping a deep drainage ditch to your right. A few hundred metres later, a waymarked wooden footbridge crosses the ditch to the right to emerge at the bottom of a large, tree-lined field.

Head uphill, alongside the field edge. At the top of the slope, follow the field boundary as it bends to the left around the corner of the woods. Glance back here, and you'll see the distant Mersey framed by wooded hills. Among the trees to the left here is Queen Charlotte's Wood **Scout Camp** **10**. Continue on the well-used path that sweeps gently uphill around the margins of the next two fields, to emerge through a kissing-gate on Commonside Lane.

Cross the road to another signposted kissing-gate opposite. From here, the path curves uphill to the right, above black-and-white Cliff Farm, before continuing beneath the wooded slopes of **Alvanley Cliff** **11**. Suddenly,

Alvanley Cliff *Looking north from the Trail below wooded Alvanley Cliff the panorama takes in Helsby Hill, the Mersey Estuary and the distant Welsh hills*

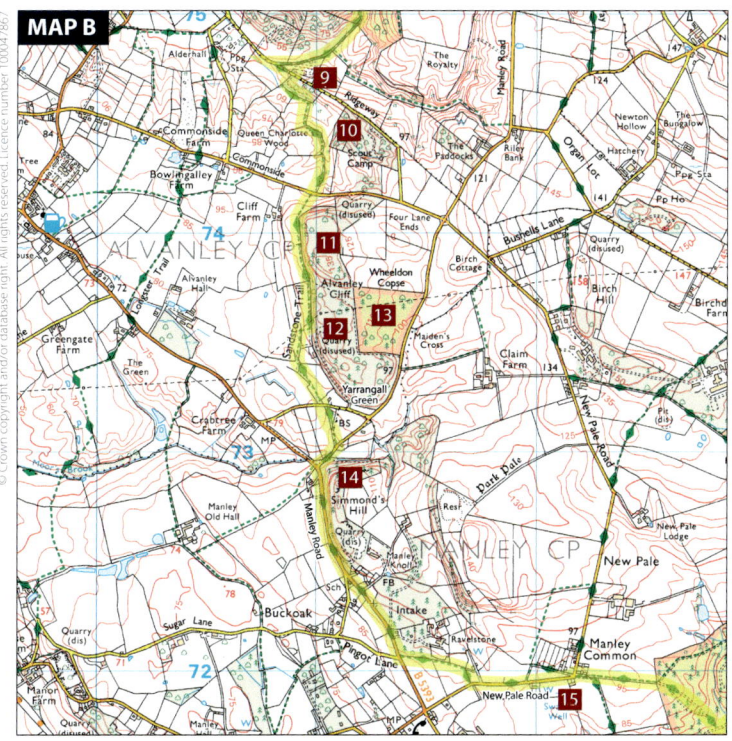

the view opens out: behind you are the Mersey Estuary and Helsby Hill, and away to the right, the patchwork of the Cheshire Plain backed by the Welsh mountains. For the next half kilometre, the level path traverses the top of fields at the base of the cliff. Compare the sandstone crags jutting from the slopes above with the occasional pale, ice-worn glacial boulders built into the field walls beside the path.

Beyond overhead power lines, the Trail zigzags right and left around the paddocks of ancient, half-timbered **Austerson Old Hall** 12. For the best view of the house, look back through hedgerow damson trees from the bottom of the slope. Fifty metres on, bear left through a kissing gate and follow the fenced path to the lane beside Yarrangall Green Farm.

(For a short but worthwhile summer detour to the wildflower meadows at **Wheeldon Copse** 13, turn left here, and then left again, onto Manley Road. The meadow, on the left 300 metres later, is old common land now designated as Access Land, and open to anyone on foot.)

Cross the narrow lane and continue straight ahead on a short path that drops gently across two fields to Manley Road, at the foot of wooded **Simmond's Hill** 14. Turn right, and walk along the verge for a hundred metres to a T-junction. Cross the sometimes busy road and turn left, uphill, towards Manley and Tarvin. For the next kilometre or so, the Trail follows the safe, tarmaced roadside pavement. Continue past a seat at a lay-by. When the road forks beside Manley School, 500 metres on, bear left along the B5393 Tarvin road. (Manley Farm Shop is a short distance down the road to the right.) Beyond a private road to Manley Knoll, walk on past tiny, roadside

Nature Notes

Early photographs show Frodsham Hill remained bare until the 1930s and '40s. Constant browsing by cattle and sheep and accidental fires prevented the natural succession from heather and scrub to woodland. Most of the trees that clothe the slopes today have grown up since the Second World War; the Woodland Trust has actively planted other areas. The broadleaved woods clinging to the steep scarp shelter small mammals and birds, which in turn attract predatory foxes, tawny owls and sparrowhawks. Beneath the trees, blue-violet bluebells spangle the woodland floor in spring, interspersed with the green fountains of broad buckler fern.

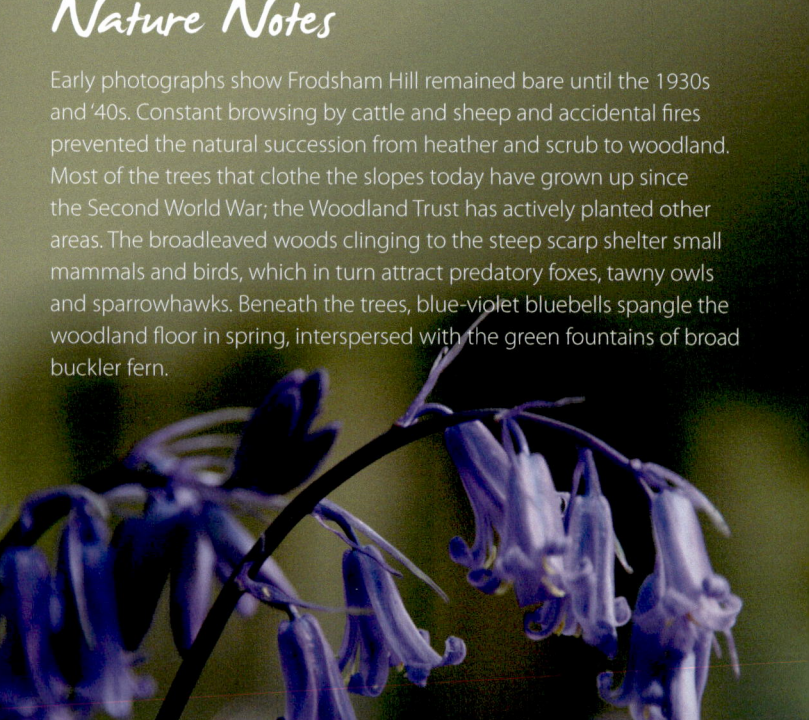

Moving house? *Austerson Old Hall is a genuine 15th-century timber-framed manor house dismantled and moved here from Nantwich, in Cheshire, in the 1970s*

St John's Church. Opposite Pingot Lane, turn left through a kissing-gate set in a drystone wall.

Away from the road, the path traces the field edge. Hidden among trees to the left, is black-and-white Ravelstone House. Through a kissing gate in the field corner, turn right, across a small paddock, onto Manley Common Road. Then turn left, past Stonehouse Farm.

(Alternatively, for refreshments and the station at Mouldsworth (1 kilometre), turn right, along New Pale Road).

Roughly 200 metres beyond the farm, look over a field gate on the left: across the field in the hedgerow is a tall standing stone. Nearby, on the verge beside a narrow access lane to cottages on the left, is a round-topped Sandstone Trail milestone. Continue along **New Pale Road** 15 to the sharp bend at Manley Common. Cross over here, and continue straight ahead on a broad footpath signposted to 'Delamere Forest'.

Cheshire County Council bought 1.6 hectare/4 acre **Ridgeway Wood** **9** in the mid 1970s to create a missing link in the newly extended Sandstone Trail. Today the mature broadleaved woodland and its plentiful dead wood support a wealth of insects and insect-eating birds. Watch and listen for lesser and greater spotted woodpeckers, nuthatches and treecreepers. In early summer the woodland floor is awash with bluebells.

Owned by the Scout Association, Queen Charlotte's Wood **Scout Camp** **10** is a 3.5 hectare/9 acre woodland campsite popular for its easy access to Delamere Forest and the Sandstone Trail. Facilities include a centrally heated log cabin with kitchen and activity room, and an outdoor camping field for up to 150 people with log seats and raised altar fires.

Until 1812 when the medieval hunting grounds were 'disafforested', Maiden Cross, near **Alvanley Cliff** **11**, marked the western edge of Delamere Forest. Before that, there were few towns, villages or churches anywhere in the heart of the old forest. The open farmland to the east was slowly reclaimed from the forest after 1812; until then much of the area was open lowland heath covered with heather, ling, bilberry and gorse.

Austerson Old Hall **12** is a surprise newcomer to Alvanley. For centuries, the Grade II listed, 15th century, three-storey jettied timber-frame farmhouse stood 44 kilometres/27 miles away at Coole Pilate near Nantwich, in Cheshire. But when a Chester architect spotted the derelict building, he had it dismantled, moved and lovingly reassembled here, below Alvanley Cliff. The work took twelve years from 1974 to 1986.

Austerson Old Hall, below Alvanley Cliff

Wheeldon Copse 13 is a new wildflower meadow created by Landlife, the environmental charity, for The Woodland Trust, with open access for everyone. The 6.5 hectare/16 acre south-facing field on the sandstone ridge is close to the Sandstone Trail. Deep ploughing to recreate 'unimproved' low-fertility soil conditions has allowed meadow flowers to flourish alongside woodland and glade species. As one delighted Alvanley resident said, 'I have never seen anything like it in 60 years'.

Until the early 1900s, when it was planted with trees, **Simmond's Hill** 14 was a bare, bracken-covered rise pitted with old stone quarries. Those at Manley Knoll produced some of the finest hard pale sandstone in Cheshire, used for the original Eaton Hall and to rebuild Chester Castle. Later, the abandoned quarries are said to have concealed illegal cockfights.

Manley old school, below Simmond's Hill

Look carefully at the Ordnance Survey map close to **New Pale Road** 15 at Manley Common, and you'll see the oval outline of a 17th century deer park. First shown on a plan of Delamere Forest dated 1627, the New Pale was a ditched and paling-fenced enclosure created under license from the King and stocked with wild deer from the forest.

Neolithic flint blade found on the ridgeway, near Woodhouse Hill

Section 2: Manley Common to Gresty's Waste

Distance:	4 miles/6.5 kilometres
Duration:	Allow 2-2½ hours
Difficulty:	Easy: Gently undulating forest tracks and field paths
Parking:	Beside New Pale Road, Manley Common
Refreshments:	Stonehouse Farm B&B and café, Manley, Carriers Inn, Hatchmere; Station Café, Delamere; café at Linmere Visitor Centre; pubs in Kelsall

Outline: *Through Delamere Forest Park: woodland tracks and paths, dappled shade, flooded mossland, hunting lodge, Pale Heights, panoramic views, Iron Age hillfort, medieval quarry, Roman road, turnpike tollhouse.*

MAP C The small settlement of Manley Common sits on a sharp bend on New Pale Road. Close to the apex of the bend is a path and bridleway signposted to 'Delamere Forest'; it begins alongside a row of concrete houses and runs between hedges out across the fields. Over a slight rise, 400 metres on, the path drops gently downhill, between posts, into the modern margins of **Delamere Forest** 16. Go straight ahead on the well-used, waymarked path that snakes downhill beneath a stand of mature Scots pines — home to Manley Hill Bike Park's downhill mountain bike and timber trails.

▲ *Nettleford Wood*

Section two: *Manley Common to Gresty's Waste* 49

At the bottom of the slope, turn left at the T-junction, onto a broad forest track signposted to 'Beeston Castle'. Over a stream, the path bends to the left. Ignoring side paths to the right and left, continue uphill on a curving, waymarked path between tree-topped banks.

At the top of the slope, some 400 metres later, is a major crossing of paths. Bear right on the forest track, and immediately left, onto a waymarked, narrower, rising path between younger trees.

Within 100 metres, the short path arrives at an angled T-junction with staggered timber barriers; bear left here, on the broader, surfaced, forest

lodges' access track. The track curves to the left and then runs straight on between closely ranked conifers. Beyond a slight rise, the track dips downhill to the right; immediately after a fenced culvert and before the T-junction here, turn right, on a narrow waymarked path that rises gently beneath overhanging trees.

At the top of the slope, less than 30 metres on, continue straight ahead across a broad, undulating forest track and cycle path. The surfaced path ahead sweeps progressively to the right around the inside edge of the forest, with the open fields of Houndslough- and Pinewood Farms out to the left.

When the path forks beside a bench, 400 or so metres on, bear right, on the better-used, waymarked path that curves away from the forest edge. Soon the track broadens to become a limestone-chipping surfaced forest timber extraction road. At the next junction, continue straight ahead. Half a kilometre on, bear right at a Sandstone Trail milestone to emerge through a metal barrier onto the main, Ashton Road (better known locally as the 'Switchback Road') through Delamere Forest Park.

Autumn mists *Caught in a shaft of sunlight, a walker enjoys a quiet moment in Delamere Forest*

(The small, lakeside settlement of Hatchmere, roughly 1.5 kilometres to the east, offers a shop, café, pub and restaurant. Turn left and follow the 'switchback road' through the forest to Hatchmere crossroads.)

Cross the often busy Ashton or 'switchback' road ⚠ in the heart of Delamere Forest Park, to the Barnsbridge Gates car park opposite. The roadside Sandstone Trail information board here displays maps and details of the route, transport and updates. Go past a metal barrier to the right of the car park, and follow the signposted track into the trees towards 'Whitchurch'. For the first half kilometre, stands of mature sweet chestnuts fringe the track and in October strew their edible nuts across the Trail.

Three hundred metres later, the track bends to the right; on the left here is a lesser path that offers a brief diversion to vast, flooded **Blakemere Moss 17** Continue on the main path to a major crossroads of forest tracks with massive timber waymarkers on either side. Go straight ahead here, on a broad track beneath tall beeches. When the track curves sharply around to the right, 200 metres later, continue straight ahead on the narrower, waymarked path that curves gently uphill to the left, to cross the **Chester-Manchester railway line 18** on a broad iron and stonework bridge.

Exploring **Delamere Forest**

Delamere Forest 16 is all that remains of four vast forests that once dominated medieval Cheshire: Wirral, Macclesfield, *Mara* (known as *de la Mara* from around 1200), and *Mondrem*. None of these forests are mentioned in the Domesday Book. The Normans simply created them during the late 11th and early 12th centuries as royal hunting grounds where the king and his earls could indulge their passion for the 'chase'. In other words, medieval 'forest' was little more than a legal entity granting the king exclusive hunting rights within its boundaries.

Furthermore, what the Norman's called 'forest' was very different from Delamere today. There were no close ranked conifer plantations. There wasn't even much dense woodland. Medieval forests were more about venison than trees. Red, fallow and roe deer, and wild boar filled the Forest. Although much of the land was undoubtedly wooded, a great deal was also unenclosed 'waste', mossland, or heath—covered in heather, ling, bilberry, gorse, bracken and birch scrub—dotted with occasional villages and scattered farms.

The 'Delamere Horn'— the 12th century badge of office of the Master Forester

By the fourteenth century, the twin forests of Delamere and Mondrem covered much of central Cheshire, stretching from the Mersey down to Nantwich, and from the Gowy across to the Weaver. An ancient road called Peytefinsty, linking Tarporley and Weaverham, separated the two forests. But as the centuries passed, the forests shrank; Mondrem was gradually reclaimed for agriculture; and by 1627, only Delamere remained.

Fierce forest law protected the Earl of Chester's precious 'vert and venison'. Hunting was forbidden except to the privileged few; and there were big fines for the illegal extraction of timber, land clearance, or cattle grazing. The Forest was run by a hereditary Master Forester, supported by eight under foresters and two grooms, or garçons. The Master Forester lived in the 'Chamber in the Forest', a sandstone lodge on top of the Old Pale; while the under foresters worked from smaller lodges, such as Eddisbury Lodge, scattered strategically throughout the Forest.

> *"Delamere Forest: 1,000 years of hunting, timber and leisure"*

Horse-drawn gypsy caravans, or 'vardos', were once a common sight in Delamere Forest

Like modern game reserves, Delamere was particularly rich in wildlife, too. Early records mention: 'Foxes, heires, cattes, weesels and other vermin; sparhawkes, marlins, hobbys, and swarmes of bees'. As well as wild cats, other contemporary animals included pine martens and polecats; while wolf packs hunted among the trees well into the fourteenth century. As late as 1656, a chronicler could still write: 'Besides the great store of deer, both red and fallow, there is also great plenty of hares, also great plenty of conies [rabbits] both black and grey. Neither do it lack foxes, otters, partridges, woodcock, plovers, ravens, crows, choughs, kites and such like.'

But when the last deer were hunted out during the Civil War, the emphasis changed to money making. Rights were sold by the Crown to take wood, peat, turves, sand and gravel from the forest. Delamere was officially 'disafforested' in 1812 after a statement called it 'a district which now produces nothing but heath, affording a scanty subsistence to a few sheep and rabbits'. By 1823, over 3,500 acres had been planted with oaks intended to provide timber for the British Navy; the rest was gradually reclaimed for agriculture by large-scale marling. But when the oaks failed to produce useful timber, the Forestry Commission replaced them with close-ranked conifers in the years following the First World War.

Delamere Forest was officially declared a Forest Park in 1987; and today it's managed as much for people and wildlife as it is for timber.

Sunny Avenue *Wandering along the grassy ridgeway beneath the trees at Eddisbury on a summer's afternoon*

Go straight ahead at a junction of paths in a dip. At the top of the rise, continue ahead on a narrow, waymarked path between wooden posts. Beyond the farm buildings and paddocks of picturesque **Eddisbury Lodge 19**, the path emerges onto a broad sandy lane.

(There is a Delamere Forest Visitor Centre with a café, toilets and bike hire less than a kilometre to the east; nearby is 'Go Ape', an innovative, aerial high-wire adventure. Half a kilometre farther on is Delamere Station House café. To reach them, turn left and follow the sandy lane towards the Forestry Depot.)

For the Sandstone Trail, turn left along the lane, and then almost immediately right, up a curving drive beneath mature trees, signposted to 'Nettleford Wood'. (Off to the right is Grey's Gate, an old entrance to the forest.) The drive snakes uphill with paddocks and horse jumps on either side. Past white-painted Eddisbury Lodge Cottage, the grassy track rises gently beneath an avenue of tall sycamores. Up to the left are the steep slopes of Pale Heights topped by a trio of communications masts and a disused underground Civil Defence bunker.

Go through the wooden kissing-gate ahead to enter Nettleford Wood. For the next short section of the Sandstone Trail, there are two alternative routes.

Stone circle *Stunning views from the summit of Pale Heights give a 270° panorama taking in Delamere Forest, the Mersey estuary, the Welsh hills and the Pennines*

The original route continues straight ahead on a pleasant path through the woods. Alternatively, turn left, uphill on the signposted route, which ascends the slopes of **Pale Heights** [20] between bands of native trees. Towards the summit, bear right, on a surfaced path that traverses the slopes below the masts. (Alternatively, to fully appreciate the panoramic views, bear left on a broad, chipping-surfaced path that rises to the summit, north of the communication masts. A circular, stone-plinthed toposcope here looks out over Delamere Forest and Blakemere below. Away to the west are the distinctive hills of the Clwydian Range, to the north, the Mersey, to the east, the distant Pennines. In the middle distance to the southeast are the ridge-top earthworks of **Eddisbury hillfort** [21].)

Less than 20 metres later, bear right, on a waymarked path through a gap in the old field hedge. The path skirts the lip of a steep slope before dropping downhill to the right again, through another old field boundary, to re-enter Nettleford Wood at the base of the slope.

Back on the original Trail, turn left, inside the woodland edge again, and continue gently downhill beneath the trees on a broad track signposted to 'Gresty's Waste' and 'Primrose Hill'. Shortly afterwards, look out for a twin-headed, steel and ceramic sculptured boar beside the path: one of its tusked snouts points north to 'Frodsham', the other south, on towards 'Whitchurch'.

The track curves downhill to the left, around Hangingstone Hill and an ancient, disused quarry called **King's Chair** 22 hidden among the trees. Continue past a side path on the left, signposted to 'Stoney Lane', which roughly coincides with the route of **Watling Street** 23—the ancient Roman military road from Chester to Manchester. Beyond a metal barrier, the track emerges at the old turnpike **tollbar cottage** 24—now a cream-painted cottage called 'Kelsall Lodge'—beside the main A54.

Taking great care ⚠, cross the busy A54 to a path into wooded Gresty's Waste, directly opposite.

Nature Notes

The Old Pale has recently been replanted with trees more than 600 years after it was first cleared from the medieval forest in 1337. A hundred and thirty seven hectares/340 acres of former farmland bought by the Forestry Commission in December 2000 is currently being developed in partnership with Mersey Forest as mixed coniferous and broadleaved community woodland. The open rides and meadows support at least 15 species of butterfly, including meadow brown, wall brown, gatekeeper, and small copper. Yet despite this success, enlightened ecologists suggest a real opportunity was missed to recreate declining lowland heath habitat on these hills.

Originally one of over forty boggy areas, or 'mosses', shown on the Crown Estate map of Delamere, **Blakemere Moss** 17 was drained and planted with trees between 1793 and 1815 to provide timber for the Royal Navy's warships. Two centuries later, in 1997, Forest Enterprise clear felled 46 hectares/113 acres of the old peat land and is letting it re-flood naturally. Today, the new wetland provides superb habitat for water birds and dragonflies.

The first section of the **Chester-Manchester railway line** 18 opened from Northwich to Mouldsworth in 1869; and the line had reached Chester by 1874. By 1905, Delamere Station had its own stationmaster, clerks, porters and signalmen to cope with eight trains a day in each direction. Together with extra seasonal excursions from Manchester and Birkenhead, the passenger services brought hordes of urban visitors to enjoy the forest.

In medieval times, the head forester had eight underforesters and two garçons, or grooms, to help him. One of these lived in **Eddisbury Lodge** 19. His job was to protect the 'beasts of the chase': red, roe and fallow deer, and wild boar. He also helped enforce fierce forest law, which prohibited the carrying of bows and arrows, while killing or injuring the 'beasts' was occasionally punishable by mutilation or death.

In 1337, the Black Prince ordered his head forester to enclose some 180 hectares/450 acres of land around Eddisbury hillfort to preserve 'vert and

Delamere Station's numerous staff around 1905

venison'. Known as the Old Pale, the enclosure later housed a stone lodge called the 'Chamber in the Forest'. Climb to the top of **Pale Heights** 20 today and you'll discover what an excellent lookout it must have been in the daily battle against poachers.

The earliest, largest and most complex of the defended settlements along the sandstone ridge, **Eddisbury hillfort** 21 was built in the late Bronze or early Iron Age to control the strategic crossroads where the ridgeway met the Kelsall Gap. Roman legionaries destroyed the fort, which lay derelict until King Alfred's daughter, Aethelfleada, rebuilt Eddisbury as a defended burgh against marauding Danes. Excavations in 1935-8 uncovered pottery, stone hammers, a bronze mirror and iron comb.

The overgrown **King's Chair** 22 quarry cut into the side of Hangingstone Hill, just off the Trail in Nettleford Wood, is the reputed source of the sandstone used to build Vale Royal Abbey between 1277 and 1300. Others suggest it was first quarried by the Romans to surface their road. The fford part of Nettle-ford is Celtic/Welsh for a track or way; but does it refer to the prehistoric ridgeway or the old native track over the ridge adopted by the Roman road?

A section of **Watling Street** 23—the Roman road between Chester (*Deva*) and Manchester (*Mamucium*)—can still be explored in Nettleford Wood and Organsdale Field, above the modern A51, near Kelsall. When the Romans left, these ancient roads remained in use for over a thousand years. Excited Victorian antiquarians who excavated a short section in 1885 claimed to have found 'one of the most remarkable sections of Roman road in Britain'.

Turnpikes were Britain's first private toll roads. When the Chester to Northwich turnpike was built in 1769, it adopted a slightly lower route through the Kelsall Gap than the old Roman road. The original **tollbar cottage** 24 still survives beside the modern A51 at Gresty's Waste. Typical tolls included: cows, a farthing, horses, a penny, and coaches, sixpence—while farm carts and funerals passed for free.

Roman Watling Street excavations, Eddisbury, 1885

Section 3: Gresty's Waste to Tarporley

Distance:	5 miles/8 kilometres
Duration:	Allow 2-3 hours
Difficulty:	Easy-Moderate: Undulating forest tracks, green lanes and field paths
Parking:	Gresty's Waste car park on the A54
Refreshments:	Pubs and shops in Kelsall; Boot Inn, Boothsdale; Rose Farm Shop and Café, John Street, Utkinton; pubs and cafés in Tarporley

Outline: *Southern outlier of Delamere Forest, glacial features, panoramic views, green lanes, spring and lost well, old quarry, undulating farmland, marl pits, site of historic Tarporley Racecourse.*

MAP D From the dedicated car park on the A54 at Gresty's Waste, take the signposted path that enters the trees alongside the Sandstone Trail notice board. A separate sign warns, 'This Car Park is locked one hour after dusk'. Nearby is a gap in the roadside fence: the crossing point for walkers arriving from Delamere Forest Park. The path drops down a long flight of steps, beneath pines, into a steep sided valley called **Hindswell Gutter** [25]. Cross

▲ *Sandy Lane*

Section three: *Gresty's Waste to Tarporley* 61

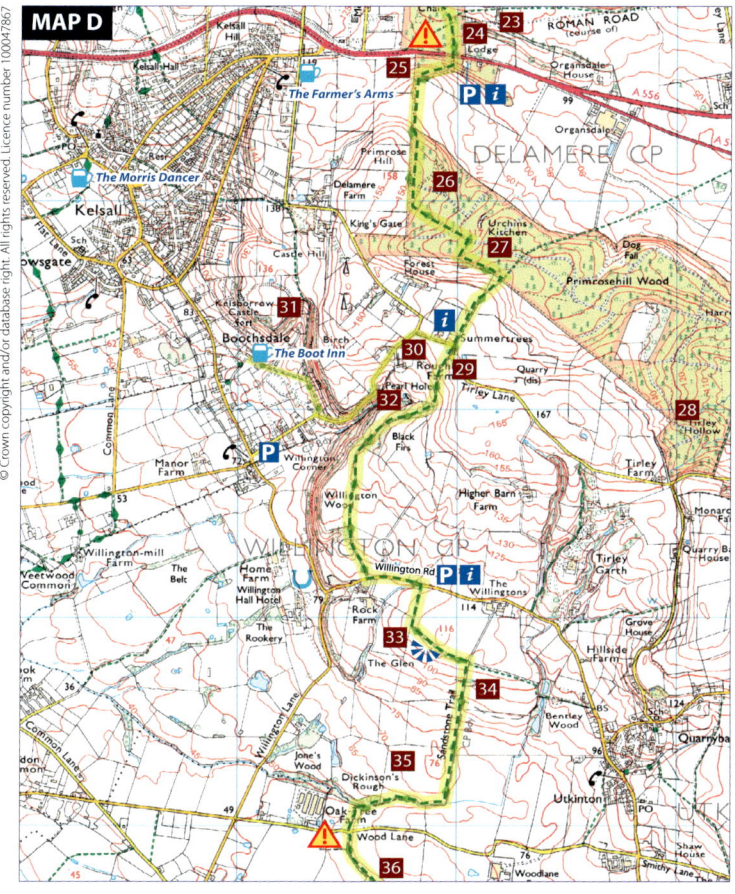

the wooden footbridge over the streambed at the bottom, turn right, and ascend the opposite slope through the trees.

At the top, the path bears left through a narrow isthmus of Scots pine and beeches straddling the ridge. Broad views open out to the east, spanning the old, so-called New Pale, ancient Eddisbury hillfort and the route of the Roman road, framed by the modern margins of Delamere Forest Park. The path meanders between huge sandstone boulders cleared here over the

Hidden gorge *Deep in Primrosehill Wood is Urchin's Kitchen, a curious glacial meltwater channel gouged through the sandstone towards the end of the last Ice Age*

centuries from nearby fields. Beyond crossing farm access tracks, the path ascends into **Primrosehill Wood 26**. Once among the trees, the Trail zigzags left and then right on a gently rising path between coniferous plantations. Continue straight ahead, ignoring two lesser paths off to the left. At a fork, bear left, downhill, on the main waymarked path.

When the sandy path meets a broad, surfaced forest track at the bottom of the slope, go straight ahead, following a fingerpost for the 'Sandstone Trail'. (Uphill to the right is King's Gate, one of the traditional entrances to the forest.) Less than 50 metres on, at the bottom of the dip, turn sharp right onto a narrower rising path signposted to 'Beeston'.

(Directly opposite this bend, a narrow woodland path heads into the trees. Look for the interpretive panel beside the Trail. It's well worth making a brief detour here to visit the mysterious glacial drainage channel of **Urchin's Kitchen 27**.)

At the forest edge, less than 100 metres later, turn left and continue uphill on the waymarked Sandstone Trail. The path climbs gently with steep pastures on the right. Close to the top of the slope, in part of the forest called Colonel's Hatch, look out for another waymarker post on the left. Turn right here, up the field bank on a short flight of steps, and through a metal kissing-gate beneath tall sycamore trees.

(Along the forest edge, 1 kilometre/½ mile to the southeast is the lost site of **Whistlebitch Well 28**, a mineral spring once accredited with miraculous healing powers.)

Out in open farmland now, the path follows the hedgeline uphill. On the brow of the slope, 100 metres later, go right, through another kissing-gate, and continue along the far side of the hedge to the left.

Beyond two more kissing-gates, the path emerges on Tirley Lane at another old entrance to the forest once known as Walley's Gate.

Out on Tirley Lane, go straight ahead on the 'S' bend, keeping to the roadside verge. This area is called Birch Hill. New views to the west and the Welsh hills open out ahead, beyond a small circular dew pond in the field to the right. Less than 50 metres later, as Tirley Lane snakes sharply to the left, turn right, off the road, down a narrow path signposted to 'Beeston Castle'. Called **Sandy Lane 29**, this delightful, winding green lane drops gently downhill for the next 1.5 kilometres towards Willington Lane. Narrow and hemmed in at first by high banks, the lane is bright with flowers in spring, and a real haven for wildlife. (Out to the right, across the sloping fields, is **Roughlow Farm 30**; and beyond it, hidden behind a rise on the far side of the valley, the Iron Age promontory fort of **Kelsborrow Castle 31**.) Within 500 metres, the lane widens and sweeps to the right around the deep, wooded hollow of **Pearl Hole 32**. For the next kilometre, the lane loops around the contours, with narrow Willington Wood hugging the lip of the slope across the fields to the right.

Beyond the far end of Willington Wood, Sandy Lane finally comes out onto Willington Road, opposite Rock Farm.

Follow the fingerpost towards 'Beeston Castle' and turn left along Willington Road. Walk along the grassy verge for 200 metres to a Sandstone Trail information board beside the second of two roadside lay-bys.

Kelsall's **Hindswell Gutter** 25 is a glacial valley formed by both the advancing and then the retreating ice sheet during the last, Devensian Ice Age, between 22,000 and 18,000 years ago. The large fields nearby were scrubby heathland until 1860-4 when 220 hectares/540 acres were reclaimed for farming by spreading thousands of tons of limey clay called marl. Seventy men and boys working with horse-drawn wagons on rails could reclaim 12 hectares/30 acres a month.

Poor sandy soil and shallow rocky outcrops have determined the uses of **Primrosehill Wood** 26 over the centuries. As part of the royal hunting forest, the area was largely open heath. Oak, larch and Scots pine were planted from 1812-1839 to provide timber for the British navy. But when the scheme failed in 1848 much of the area was reclaimed for agriculture. Today, the slopes are largely clad in Forestry Commission conifers.

Hidden by trees, atmospheric **Urchin's Kitchen** 27 is another glacial drainage channel formed towards the close of the last Ice Age. The 6-9 metre/20-30 feet deep, meandering water-worn gorge is wider at the base than the top—which suggests it was probably scoured out under immense pressure beneath a huge but unknown depth of ice. The gorge was used as a cart road in the past. Urchin is an old Cheshire dialect word that means both 'hedgehog' and, more probably, 'devil'.

Local children outside Kelsall post office, around 1910

Long lost **Whistlebitch Well** 28 at the far end of Primrosehill Wood was once a famous Elizabethan health spa. A rare pamphlet in the British Museum entitled 'Newes out of Cheshire of the new-found well' describes how, in the early 1600s, its fame spread until 'greater and greater multitudes' of the sick and curious were visiting, 'even unto two thousand a daie'. Its original name, *Twiselbache*, means the 'forked stream'.

Sandy Lane 29 is a lovely sunken green lane that meanders for over a kilometre gently downhill from the old entrance to the forest at Walley's Gate, on Tirley Lane, to Rock Farm, on Willington Lane below. Its steep, hedged banks provide ideal habitat for mice, voles, rabbits and nesting birds, and their predators: weasels, stoats and foxes. In spring and summer, the lane is awash with wildflowers.

Seventeenth century pamphlet describing Whistlebitch Well

Cheshire's open sandstone ridge and light sandy upland soil attracted prehistoric travellers and settlers. **Roughlow Farm** 30 is named after a nearby Bronze Age burial mound, tumulus or 'low'. Less than two kilometres to the east, on Fishpool Road, is Seven Lows Farm. Many other local burial mounds have been 'ploughed out' in the last century or so, including: Coblow, Garraslow, Hounslow, Kelsborrow, Oulton Low, Rulow, Wanslow Well and Willow Wood.

Reputedly once named 'Celts' barrow' after a nearby burial mound, **Kelsborrow Castle** 31 is a small, oval, late Bronze Age/early Iron Age promontory fort perched on the western flank of the sandstone ridge, above Kelsall. A single eroded rampart, once topped by a wooden palisade, protects the flat ground to the north. A bronze axe head and fragment of an iron sword were found here in 1810.

The porous sandstone of the Cheshire ridge acts like a giant sponge, and has provided drinking water from springs and wells since time immemorial. **Pearl Hole** 32 is an ancient spring whose name derives from an Old English word *pyrle*, meaning a 'bubbling stream'. For centuries, it was the sole water source for local cottages; today, a reservoir set into the slope supplies Willington below.

MAP E Cross the road 50 metres later, and turn right, through a kissing gate beside an arch-topped Sandstone Trail milestone that reads 'Willington Road – Frodsham 18km, Whitchurch 37km'.

Go straight ahead on a field path that rises gently uphill beside the hedge. At the crest of the hill go through a kissing gate. The view suddenly opens out to reveal one of the best panoramas on the Trail so far. In fact, the next 20 kilometres of the route are laid out in front of you. Ahead, to the south, is the striking and distinctive, castle-topped **Beeston Crag** 33 — the defining centrepiece of the Sandstone Trail. Beyond it, stretching away to the southwest, lie the wooded hills and rust-red cliffs of Cheshire's central sandstone ridge. The dramatic Welsh hills span the horizon to the west.

Turn left. The path hugs the top of the slope with the hawthorn-topped sandstone field bank to the left. Look out for occasional large glacial erratic boulders cleared here from the fields. Beyond a slight rise, go through a foot gate and drop, right, into a broad, hedge-lined farm lane. Ignore the path directly ahead, which leads to the small settlement of Utkinton, visible on the slope ahead.

The farm lane falls steeply downhill between tall hedges festooned with brambles. Halfway down the slope, behind the hazel and blackthorn hedge on the left, is a small, overgrown and flooded quarry, known to locals by the curious name of the **Swimming Pool** **34**.

When the lane opens out into a vast, **undulating field** **35**, continue straight ahead and follow the hedgeline downhill. For the next 1.5 kilometres, to the end of Old Gypsy Lane, the Trail sticks to the old parish boundary between Willington and Utkinton.

At the very bottom of the slope, bear right, alongside the stream. Just before the far corner of the field, turn left, across a clearly waymarked wooden footbridge. On the far bank, turn right, keeping to the field boundary, now

Winter farmland *Two well-wrapped winter walkers on the Sandstone Trail follow the old parish boundary up the slope towards Willington*

Green lane *Once a favourite stopping place for Romany travellers, Old Gypsy Lane is notable today for its wealth of wildflowers and butterflies*

with the stream on the right. Beyond Dickinson's Rough, bear left around the far end of the field, to emerge on tree-lined Wood Lane. Listen carefully here, and you should be able to hear the thousands of intensively bred turkeys at nearby Oak Tree Farm.

Cross the road with care ⚠ and go through a kissing-gate opposite, signposted to 'Beeston Castle'. For the next 600 metres, the Trail meanders along an ancient green lane. Known locally as **Old Gypsy Lane 36**, its western ditch marks the parish boundary between Willington and Utkinton. When the lane curves to the right, beyond a simple wooden bench, bear left through a waymarked kissing gate. Beyond another, 150 metres on, bear right through a kissing gate and then left around the outside edge of lovely **Oxpasture Wood 37**.

Beyond two further gates beside a small pond, a Sandstone Trail fingerpost points diagonally across the long field ahead towards a yellow waymarked post in the far, righthand corner. The path emerges at a junction of farm tracks beside a pond and cluster of isolated cottages at **Fishers Green** 38.

Turn left and then immediately right, on a broad, surfaced farm track signposted to 'Beeston Castle'. Called **Gullet Lane** 39, the track meanders south with open pastures on either side, then narrows and runs on beneath oaks and ashes. When the lane ends, go through a kissing-gate and continue along a fenced path skirting the edge of Ash Wood. The fields out to the right here were once the site of **Tarporley Racecourse** 40. Past a partially infilled pond, the path bends to the right past private paddocks. Go through a kissing-gate, and turn left. Beyond the huge sheds of the old EU '**Buffer Depot**' 41, the Trail comes out on the busy A51 (Rode Street). Turn left along the pavement for 10 metres, past Racecourse Farm, and cross the busy A51 with great care ⚠.

Nature Notes

Central Cheshire's characteristic hedgerow oaks are home to significant numbers of little owls. These non-native birds were introduced into Cheshire from 1842 onwards; their subsequent spread was explosive. Early Cheshire records include one shot at Farndon in 1868 and another at Arley, near Northwich, in 1887. By the 1930s they were present in every county south of the Humber. Often out and about but usually inactive during the day, little owls are best seen at dusk; watch for their dumpy, upright silhouettes perched on a prominent branch or post. They can also be recognised by their low, bounding flight and odd, almost puppy-like *kwee-oo* call.

One of the Trail's loveliest panoramas opens out from the crest of the ridge above Rock Farm. To the west are the 'blue remembered hills' of Wales. To the south, in the middle distance, distinctive, castle-topped **Beeston Crag** 33 juts from the Plain. Old Cheshire weather lore says that 'When Beeston Castle wears a hood, Huxley Meadow gets a flood'.

Beeston Crag from an 18th century etching

Where the underlying sandstone pushes to the surface, two small quarries have been excavated on either side of the Trail. The deep, overgrown pool on one side is known locally as the **Swimming Pool** 34. In the past, the bottom was cemented over and one end of the pool, complete with diving board, was used to teach the Tomkinson children of nearby Willington Hall to swim.

From below the crest of the ridge to the stream, the Trail follows the Utkinton-Willington parish boundary along the edge of a vast **undulating field** 35. This typical glacial 'drift' landscape is composed of material deposited by an ancient ice sheet. Straddling the hedge is an elongated whale-shaped hill called a drumlin whose long axis is aligned with the original movement of the ice.

A green lane, known locally as **Old Gypsy Lane** 36, runs southeast from Wood Lane towards Fishers Green and Tarporley. The western hedge and ditch mark the parish boundary. The sheer variety of different tree species here suggests the lane is old; look for oak, hazel, holly, alder, elder, sallow, osier and hawthorn.

It's hard to believe that part of **Oxpasture Wood** 37 was originally a large duck pond called Dodd's Pool. But when its dam burst, the dry pool gradually

Tarporley Races from an oil painting in the Swan Hotel, Tarporley

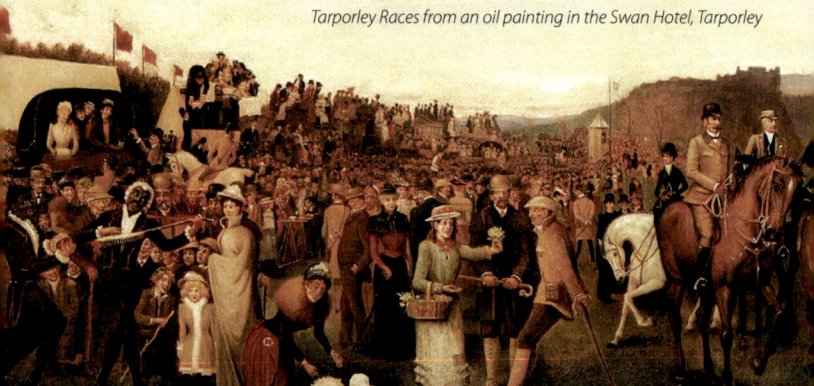

reverted to mature woodland. Although many of the broadleaved trees were later replaced with quick-growing conifers, the flush of bluebells and wood anemones here each spring is a reminder of the wood's deciduous past.

Once known as Walker's Green, **Fishers Green** 38 appears on the Enclosures Award map of 1808 as a hamlet of tiny farms clustered around two pieces of communal land, or 'greens', each with its own pond. But the greens were later enclosed, the ponds filled in, and the old lane to Clotton Common swallowed by the fields. All that remains of the 17th century settlement is Fishers Green Farmhouse with its massive central chimney.

The guttural 'gullet' in **Gullet Lane** 39 is old Cheshire dialect for a long narrow piece of land, a water channel or gulley. One of the fields alongside the lane was originally called Brick Kiln Field; the high bank halfway down Gullet Lane may be the site of the old kiln.

For over 60 years, between 1878 and 1939, the fields to the west of Gullet Lane and Ash Wood were the site of **Tarporley Racecourse** 40. Held each year on a Wednesday in April, the Tarporley Hunt Steeplechase was the largest and most fashionable event in Cheshire's sporting calendar. Races on the 3-kilometre/2 mile circular course included the Farmers' Cup, and the Members' Steeplechase —ridden for many years in full hunting costume and known as the 'Red Coat Race'.

Commonly known as the **'Buffer Depot'** 41, the huge warehouses alongside the A51 north of Tarporley were originally built as European Union intervention stores to contain excess grain and sugar grown under the Common Agricultural Policy. They now provide space for transport and other businesses.

Section 4: Tarporley to Burwardsley

Distance:	5 miles/8 kilometres
Duration:	Allow 2-3 hours (plus a visit to Beeston Castle)
Difficulty:	Moderate: Level field paths, steep climb to Beeston Castle (optional), woodland track, final ascent
Parking:	(There is NO safe parking on the A51.) To join the Trail, park in the free car park behind the Rising Sun in Tarporley, and then follow the footpaths across the fields to Back Lanes
Refreshments:	Pubs and cafés in Tarporley; Shady Oak, along the canal from Wharton's Lock; café beside Beeston Castle; Pheasant Inn, Higher Burwardsley

Outline: *Lovely green lane, deserted monastic grange, marl pits, lost medieval road, Shropshire Union Canal, River Gowy, Beeston Castle, saline spa, 'Peckforton Cyclone', Peckforton Castle, woodland tracks, hilltop inn.*

MAP F Cross the busy A51 Rode Street with great care ⚠ to a tarmacked gateway on the south side of the road opposite Racecourse Farm. Go through the kissing gate signposted to 'Beeston Castle' and turn immediately right.

▲ *Beeston Castle*

Section four: Tarporley to Burwardsley 73

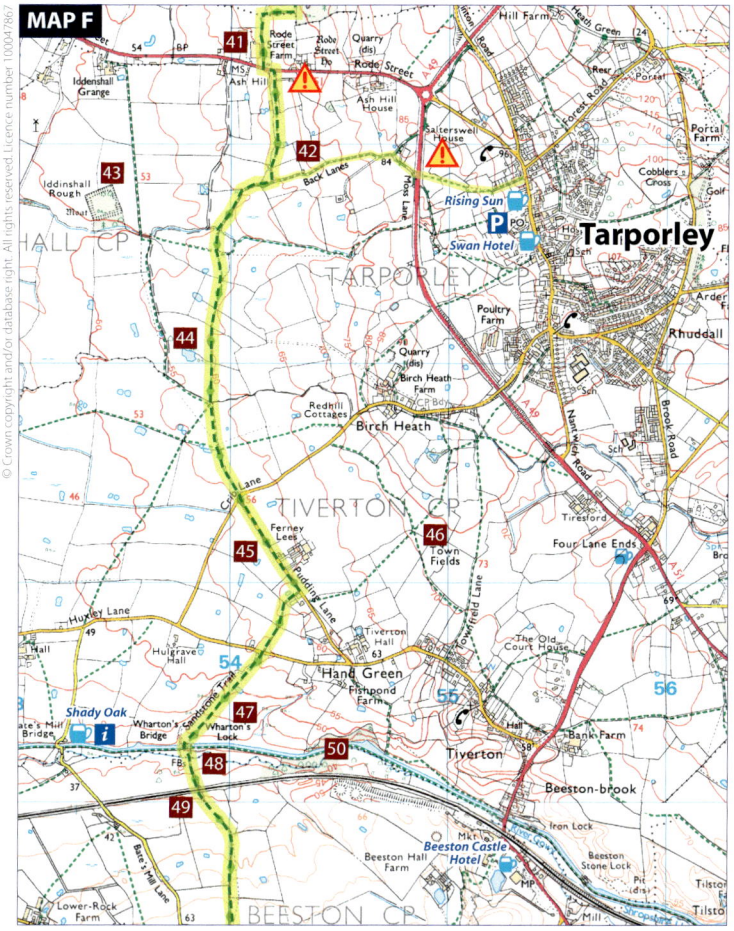

Heading away from the road now, walk up the long, narrow field towards a gateway and kissing gate in the top left-hand corner.

Continue straight ahead past a pond to another kissing gate in the top right-hand corner of the next field. Bear right across two further small irregular fields, and exit into ancient **Back Lanes** 42.

Traditional lane *Lovely Sandy Lane meanders gently downhill between Tirley Lane, on the margins of Primrosehill Wood, and Rock Farm, Willington*

(The small country town of Tarporley, roughly a kilometre to the east, offers food, drink, shops and accommodation. To reach it, turn left along Back Lanes, bear right at the fork, cross the busy by-pass ⚠, and follow the footpath across the fields to the High Street.)

To continue on the Trail, turn right along the shady green lane, flanked on either side by banks and ditches. For the next 800 metres, the path sweeps west and then southwest, around newly planted native woodland. Beyond a simple bench, the Trail crosses a wooden footbridge at the junction of two streams. Continue through a kissing-gate and bear left, around the margins of the field ahead. One field away to the west here is **Iddenshall Rough** 43—an ancient moated site hidden within a wood.

When the hedge bends to the left around the corner of the wood, 100 metres on, follow the Sandstone Trail signpost straight out across the fields towards Beeston Crag, now clearly visible ahead. Keep straight on across two large, open fields, and cross a narrow sleeper bridge over a ditch and hedge. Bear to the left across two further fields and go over a second wooden bridge. Over the ditch, the path sweeps to the left around the field boundary and runs on towards Beeston.

Beyond a wooden fingerpost beside a crossing path and cattle trough, the path continues over a waymarked footbridge in the corner of the field. The numerous small, steep-sided ponds dotting the fields ahead (and clearer still on the large scale OS Explorer map) are **marl pits 44**. Follow the hedgeline to a wooden Sandstone Trail fingerpost in midfield, and then turn left through the waymarked kissing gate. Bear right across the corner of the next field to come out, within 20 metres, on Crib Lane.

Cross over at the junction and walk down quiet **Pudding Lane 45**, ahead. Notice the distinctive black-and-white, curved topped iron railings on the corner here: they're a unique Cheshire feature now being widely restored across the county. Out to the left, behind Ferney Lees Farm, are **Tiverton Town Fields 46**, the scene of a vicious Civil War skirmish.

Nature Notes

Where the Shropshire Union Canal, River Gowy, and Crewe-Chester railway line squeeze together through the Beeston Gap, they form an important wildlife corridor and unofficial linear nature reserve. Kingfishers, water rails, mute swans, moorhens, mallard, water voles and grass snakes all live and breed along the short section of the Gowy between Beeston and Bunbury. Feral mink already hunt along the Gowy but otters have yet to make a comeback. The rough ground between the river and canal provides ideal habitat for mice, voles and shrews, which in turn support the barn owls that nest in boxes provided by the Broxton Barn Owl Group.

Tarporley's ancient **Back Lanes** 42 are arguably the loveliest section of green lane on the Sandstone Trail. The lanes may date from medieval times or earlier when monastic farmworkers walked regularly between nearby Iddenshall Grange and Tarporley Church.

Hidden among the trees at **Iddenshall Rough** 43 is the 1.6 hectare/4 acre moated site of a Saxon and medieval monastic grange that once belonged to Chester Abbey. Webb's 1622 *Itinerary of Cheshire* mentions the *'fine house and fair demesne of Idenshaw'*; pieces of dressed stone are scattered throughout the copse. The moat's large size and strategic position suggest it may also originally have been the site of an early Roman auxiliary fortlet.

According to the 17th century Cheshire writer, Daniel King, marl is *'a kind of fat clay spread upon arable land which bringeth corn in as great abundance as that which is dunged'*. This natural fertiliser was later replaced by bone dust, wood ash and guano, and finally by lime and chemical fertilisers. **Marl pits** 44 can be recognised by their regular shape and steep sides.

Pudding Lane 45 is named after a curious local incident. A large pudding was traditionally cooked for the nearby annual fair at Bunbury Wakes. When gallons of milk started to vanish from Tiverton Hall the farmer became suspicious and searched his workers' cottages. He found the missing milk hidden in a chest

The hunt meeting outside Beeston Smithy, around 1910

of drawers. When the story got out, delighted locals promptly renamed the nearby track Pudding Lane.

Just to the east of Pudding Lane are **Tiverton Town Fields** 46, the site of a fierce Civil War skirmish on the evening of 21st February, 1642. A local vicar's diary records: *'Three hundred Parliament men were met by the horse of the array on Te'erton Townfield, where one of Colonel Mainwaring's men was slain on the Parliament side and a few others on the King's, who were buried at Tarporley'.*

The Trail crosses the Shropshire Union Canal at **Wharton's Lock** 47. Created by an Act of Parliament in 1772, the Chester Canal (as it was then named) was completed as far as Beeston in 1775. By the time it linked to the Midlands' waterways in the 1820s and '30s, the new railways had arrived. The amalgamated Shropshire Union Railways and Canal Company continued to carry cargo on the canal until after the First World War.

The narrow **River Gowy** 48 rises at Peckforton Moss, just to the east of the sandstone hills, before meandering 39 kilometres/24 miles across Cheshire farmland to flow into the Mersey at Stanlow Point. This stretch is known as Beeston Brook. Traces of water-powered Wharton's Mill survive on the riverbank below Wharton's Lock.

George Stephenson, the 'Father of British Steam Railways', surveyed several routes for the **Crewe-Chester railway line** 49 between 1826 and 1836. He finally chose the Beeston Gap route for its easy gradients. Today, this quiet rural line links Crewe with Holyhead and the Irish ferries.

Civil War cannon ball found behind Tiverton Hall

Less than a kilometre east of the Trail are the artificial hills of a **Second World War underground fuel depot** 50. The vast storage tanks were part of a secret project codenamed PLUTO, or 'Pipeline Under The Ocean', which pumped 172 million gallons of fuel beneath the Channel to Allied forces during the D-Day invasion of Nazi-controlled Europe in 1944.

When Pudding Lane narrows, 50 metres later, turn right, through a kissing-gate, on a path to 'Beeston Castle'. The Trail crosses two further high-hedged fields to emerge close to a tiny, brick cottage on Huxley Lane.

Cross the road and go through the kissing-gate opposite. Continue straight ahead, keeping the stream hidden by dense scrub to the right. When the hedge kinks sharply to the right, some 200 metres on, follow the Sandstone Trail marker post out across the field. Head for the right-hand side of the overgrown marl pit ahead, and then drop downslope to **Wharton's Lock** **47**, in the bottom right-hand corner of the field. The Shropshire Union Canal, **River Gowy** **48**, and railway all squeeze through the Beeston Gap here, a stone's throw from Beeston Castle.

The Gowy marks the halfway point on the Sandstone Trail; a milestone reads: 'Wharton's Lock–Frodsham 26km, Whitchurch 29km'.

(A wooden fingerpost nearby points west along the canal to the 'Shady Oak Inn 1km' – a popular bankside pub whose gardens enjoy fine views of Beeston Crag.)

Castle rock *Medieval Beeston Castle high on its sandstone crag*

Wharton's Lock *Watching the world go by, two walkers pause on the canal bridge over the Shropshire Union Canal at Wharton's Lock, just south of Tarporley*

Cross the curved, white-painted Wharton's Lock Bridge (bridge number 108) and drop down through a kissing-gate to a sandstone and sheet-iron tractor bridge over the infant Gowy. A surfaced path climbs gently up the far slope to pass beneath the **Crewe-Chester railway line** 49 through a gated brick cattle arch.

Beyond the railway, the path heads for the left-hand end of Beeston Crag. Several fields away to the left, beside the railway line, are the artificial hills of a vast, **Second World War underground fuel depot** 50. Head for a kissing gate in the lefthand corner of the field. Continue on a fenced path and farm track to turn right, through a kissing-gate, into a lane encircling Beeston Crag.

Turn left, uphill on the lane, past black-and-white Castle Gate Farm. Continue past a single-track lane to arrive at the imposing, tower-flanked Victorian gateway to Beeston Castle. Opposite is a quiet, tree-fringed 'Pay and Display' car park.

MAP G **Beeston Castle** 51 is the centrepiece of the Sandstone Trail. Its medieval defences, caves, deep historic wells and legendary lost treasure are all good reasons for a visit, but to forgo the stunning panoramic views from the summit would be folly. Please don't miss it.

After your visit, continue along the lane that curves downhill beyond the castle entrance. Less than 100 metres on, beside the first bend, are a Sandstone Trail information board, picnic area and seasonal café. Bear right here, on a narrow path signposted to 'Whitchurch' that runs alongside the castle's stone **encircling wall** 52. The path soon veers left, away from the wall, and drops downhill beneath tall pines.

Cross Tattenhall Lane at the bottom of the slope, opposite the traditional sandstone and timber 'Tabernacle Cottage' and turn left, slightly uphill on the narrow pavement. Within 20 metres, turn right, up steps and go through a kissing-gate on a path signposted to 'Burwardsley'. The Trail bears left across the fields towards the wooded Peckforton Hills. Jutting from the trees on the skyline ahead is **Peckforton Castle** 53, a remarkably authentic Victorian copy of a medieval fortress. Out to the right, beyond the patchwork of the Cheshire Plain, the Welsh hills span the horizon.

At the far side of the field, cross the shallow stream valley on a wooden footbridge. Ignore the side paths running east and west along the stream and continue straight ahead. Halfway up the next field, turn right, through a wooden kissing-gate. Incidentally, the sign here points towards Stone House Lane—once at the heart of the curious **Peckforton Cyclone** 54. Through the gate, head diagonally across the field towards a group of large black-and-white houses tucked beneath the shelter of the hill.

In the far corner of the field, turn right, through another kissing-gate, into Horsley Lane. A Sandstone Trail fingerpost points on towards 'Burwardsley' and back to 'Beeston'. This lane was the old route to Burwardsley. Many of the old cottages here were spared from demolition or alteration by the Peckforton Estate and date back to the 16th century. Continue along the narrow, tarmacked lane past Moathouse Barn, Moathouse Farm, and the far older, half-timbered Moathouse with its ornate chimneys. Hidden within the private grounds of the next-door Bathhouse are the vestiges of a once-famous mineral spa called **Horsley Bath** 55 (*private: no public access*).

Roughly 100 metres later, turn left, off Horsley Lane, through a gate onto

Section four: *Tarporley to Burwardsley* 81

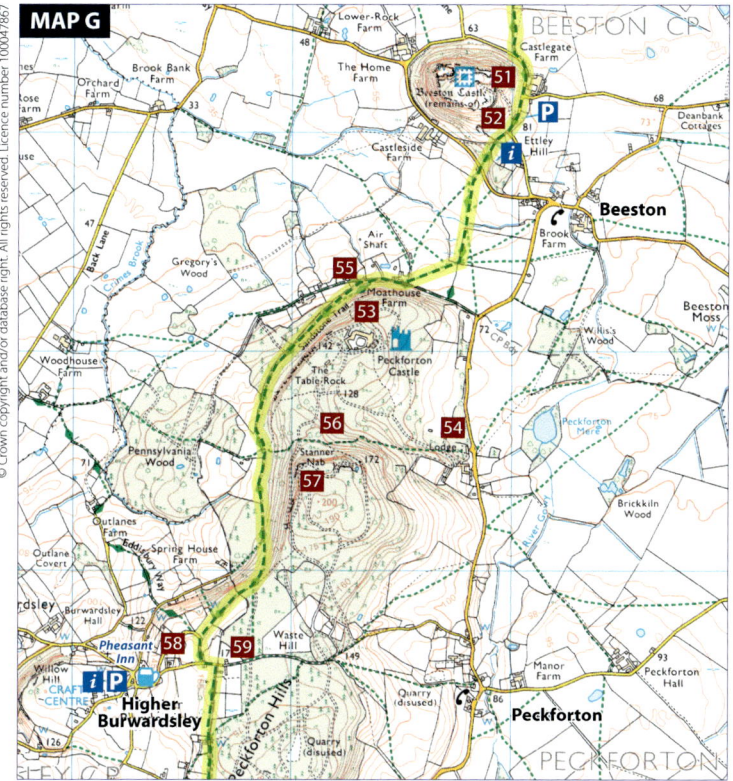

a broad track around the foot of the **Peckforton Hills 56**. For the next kilometre, the track winds gently uphill with open oak woodland clothing the steep slopes up to the left. Soon the track levels out and then drops down to a major crossroads of paths in the woods. A four-way fingerpost beside a dark yew points right to 'Pennsylvania Wood' and left, over the ridge below lofty **Stanner Nab 57**, to 'Stone House Lane'. Ignore these side paths.

The Sandstone Trail continues straight ahead, keeping to the main track around the base of the hills towards 'Burwardsley'. Beyond a few small fields out to the right, the track rises steadily alongside the trees.

When the track bends to the right and starts to drop downhill, around

Homes and castles *A cluster of genuine, half-timbered Tudor cottages survive on Horsley Lane, backed by ancient Beeston Castle*

800 metres later, turn left, up crude sandstone steps, onto a narrower path that climbs obliquely up the slope. It's clearly signposted to 'Bulkeley Hill'.

At the crest of the hill, turn right along the lip of the slope towards 'Bulkeley Hill' and 'Rawhead'. Ignore the path through the conifer plantation ahead, signposted to 'Hill Lane'. Continue through a narrow wooden picket gate between solid sandstone gateposts.

Out in the open now, the path hugs the sandstone boundary walls and hedges across two sloping fields to emerge through a kissing-gate on a narrow, curving lane. Bear left, uphill. At the T-junction, 200 metres later, beside tiny sandstone 'Rock Cottage' and 'Elephant Track Burwardsley', walkers are faced with two choices: to pause for refreshment or carry on. The fingerpost here points right, downhill, to the 'Pheasant Inn' and left, uphill, on towards 'Bulkeley Hill'.

(Just a few hundred metres downhill to the right is the charming hilltop hamlet of Higher Burwardsley, home to the attractive, upmarket real ale **Pheasant Inn** 58 . The panorama and sunsets from the pub terrace alone are worth the detour. It's the perfect place to break for a drink, a snack, full meal, or even overnight accommodation.)

Nature Notes

The well-established mixed deciduous woods on the Peckforton Hills provide superb habitat for a wealth of mammals and birds. The woodland floor teems with wood mice, shrews, and hedgehogs, along with their natural predators, the weasel, stoat, and fox. Polecats have recently returned to the woods, too. The trees support at least three species of bats; and are home to greater spotted woodpeckers, buzzards, tawny owls, wood warblers, and pied flycatchers. However, Coward, the Cheshire naturalist, wrote in 1910 that 'ring ouzels nest at the southern end of the Peckforton Hills' and 'stonechats nest annually on the Peckforton Hills.' Sadly, neither are seen today.

The stone **Encircling Wall** 52 around the base of Beeston Castle once enclosed an eighteenth century deer park belonging to Lord Tollemache of Peckforton. Built under royal license, the fifty-acre park held twenty fallow deer: both for meat and to trumpet the wealth and status of their owner.

Peckforton Castle soon after it was completed in 1851

High on Stonery Knoll stands Victorian **Peckforton Castle** 53. An authentic replica of a 13th century fortress, it was built for John (later 1st Baron) Tollemache between 1842 and 1851 for the then vast sum of £67,847 9s 7½d. Its celebrated architect, Anthony Salvin, had worked previously on Windsor Castle and the Tower of London. The castle has since appeared in an episode of the BBC TV series, 'Doctor Who', and in the 1991 film, 'Robin Hood'.

On the evening of 27th October 1913, Stonehouse Lane was battered by the freak **Peckforton Cyclone** 54. According to a contemporary eyewitness, a dark column of spinning air approached from the south, accompanied by thunder, lightning and torrential rain. During four violent hours, Castlegate

Clearing up after the 'Peckforton Cyclone', 1913

Farm lost its roof, hundreds of trees were uprooted, several cattle killed, and a local man hurled sixty metres into his neighbour's orchard.

Deep in the private grounds of Bathhouse Cottage are the remains of an 18th-century spa called **Horsley Bath** 55 Water once cascaded into a basin and then into a deep stone tank entered by steps. When the Reverend William Cole plunged in on a hot August day in 1757, he found 'the coldness of it was so extream that, trying to speak, I found it out of my power'.

Parts of the **Peckforton Hills** 56 were enclosed as a deer 'chase' on the orders of the Black Prince in 1353. Later in the Middle Ages, greyhounds hunted wild boar among the trees. Thousands of Peckforton's mature trees were requisitioned during the 1914-18 War for use in the trenches. Today's woods largely date from the wholesale post-war replantings of the 1920s.

The private viewpoint high above Peckforton Castle is called **Stanner Nab** 57. Once a favourite picnic spot for local farmers, it features a small quarry from which stone was cut for the Grosvenor Bridge in Chester. Nearby were two keepers' cottages where the 1st Baron Tollemache kept caged golden eagles.

Originally called the Leche's Arms and from 1869 the Carden Arms, the picturesque **Pheasant Inn** 58 started life as a timber-framed farmstead built in 1580. Sheltered by the hill and with its own spring, the pub probably occupies an ancient settlement site at the junction of two long-established tracks running along and across the ridge.

Sam Barnes, landlord of the Carden Arms (now the Pheasant Inn), at Burwardsley, in the 1950s

Exploring **Beeston Castle**

Beeston Castle's 51 fascinating history stretches back at least 4,000 years. The castle's isolated sandstone crag rises 112 metres/365 feet above the Cheshire Plain and is visible from both the Welsh mountains and the Pennines. There's little doubt that our distant ancestors were drawn to the hill; and one of its earliest names, Buistan, recorded in the Domesday Book, means something like 'market rock'. Neolithic stone tools have been found nearby; a Bronze Age settlement with evidence of bronze casting was excavated within the outer ward in the 1980s; and the Iron Age earthworks of a large hillfort underlie much of the medieval curtain wall, halfway up the hill. The hilltop may have had religious significance for our ancestors, too. It's easy to imagine huge Beltane fires surrounded by worshippers illuminating the summit every May Day, perhaps over several hundred years.

So when the 6th Earl of Chester, Ranulph de Blundeville chose Beeston Crag for his new castle, in 1225, the site was already ancient and important. The new castle incorporated all the state-of-the-art techniques Ranulph had witnessed during his time fighting in the Middle East during the Fifth Crusade. Beeston Castle comprises two main parts: the inner bailey with its broad rock-cut ditch,

An Edwardian postcard showing visitors to Beeston Castle around 1910

A Neolithic polished stone axe-hammer head found at the foot of Beeston Crag

massive gatehouse, circular defensive towers and deep historic well; and the larger outer bailey with its own separate well, massive gateway, ditch, and curtain wall punctuated by seven semi-circular defensive towers.

Yet medieval castles took decades to build, and neither Ranulph nor his successor lived to see its completion. Soon afterwards, Beeston was taken over by King Henry III who used it as a fortress and prison in his rekindled wars with Wales. Beeston was subsequently modified by his son, Edward I, to bring it into line with ten new fortresses built to enforce the final suppression of the Welsh.

Before King Richard II sailed from Chester to Ireland in 1399, legend says he hid his vast royal treasure in passages leading off the well at Beeston. Contemporary accounts mention '100,000 marks in gold coin, and 100,000 marks in other precious objects'. Unfortunately for generations of treasure seekers, there is evidence to suggest the treasure was captured by Henry Bolinbroke and used to pay off his supporters.

By the early 16th century, Beeston Castle had become redundant; and was described by Leland, the royal historian, as 'shattered and ruinous'. The castle was refortified during the Civil War. Three hundred Parliamentarians occupied the castle in 1643, but when a brave Royalist captain and eight of his men climbed the sheer crag at night, they managed to trick the garrison into surrendering. The Royalists then held Beeston. They were besieged for over a year, and eventually starved out. When the War ended, orders were given to dismantle the fortifications, and the castle was reduced to its current state.

Beeston Castle has been a popular local venue for fetes and day trips for centuries. Today, it's cared for by English Heritage. Facilities include the 'Castle of the Rock' exhibition, gift shop and toilets. The panoramic view from the summit reputedly spans seven old counties. The summit also makes an ideal spot for summer picnics.

> **Beeston Castle and Woodland Park**, Chapel Lane, Beeston, Cheshire, CW6 9TX, is open daily, from 10am-6pm, between April 1 and September 30; and Thursday-Monday, from 10am-4pm, between October 1 and March 31. For more information, call the ticket office direct on: 01829 260464.

Section 5: Burwardsley to Larkton Hall

Distance: 5½ miles/8.75 kilometres

Duration: Allow 2½-3½ hours

Difficulty: Moderate-Strenuous: Numerous ups and downs on this spectacular stretch

Parking: Front part (only) of the Cheshire Workshops car park, Higher Burwardsley

Refreshments: Pheasant Inn, Higher Burwardsley; Bickerton Poacher below Bickerton Hill

Outline: *Dramatic wooded hills: steep scarp slopes, stunning views to east and west, old copper mine, ancient saltway, sandstone caves, lost spring, Iron Age hillfort, rare lowland heath.*

MAP H To press on along the Sandstone Trail, turn left, uphill on Rock Lane. At the top of the slope, turn right, up steps, through a waymarked kissing-gate. The large 'Welcome to the Borough of Crewe and Nantwich' sign here marks the parish boundary. (Beyond the boundary, ahead, the tarmac peters out and ancient **Hill Lane** 59 slowly reverts to an earlier appearance.)

▲ *Sandstone Trail, Rawhead*

Follow the fenced path along the lefthand field edge. Beyond a kissing-gate, the path runs through a leafy tunnel overhung by dark holly trees. Continue past a timber-fenced paddock, and continue past two further fields, keeping to the woodland edge. The path emerges on a narrow lane.

Turn left onto Fowler's Bench Lane. The picturesque sandstone **gatehouse** 60 alongside the Peckforton Gap here belongs to the Peckforton Estate. Ignore the precipitous track ahead, which falls away to 'Stonehouse Lane'. Instead, bear right, on the broad sandy lane, signposted to 'Bulkeley Hill' and 'Rawhead'.

Less than 150 metres later, turn left, up the bank on a flight of sandstone steps into the National Trust's 'Bulkeley Hill Woods'. The path snakes uphill through open oak, birch and rowan woodland, then levels out and skirts the edge of the escarpment around **Bulkeley Hill** 61.

Soon, huge, veteran sweet chestnut trees dominate the open woodland. Close to the 'end' of Bulkeley Hill, look for the concrete base of an old winch on the lip of the slope; below it, a **narrow gauge tramline** 62 plummets down the hillside.

Follow the waymarkers as the Trail veers to the right around the end of the hill. Jutting from the edge, some 250 metres on, is a huge, flat-topped sandstone tabletop called '**Name Rock**' 63—a popular viewpoint looking east.

The path continues between iron posts in a nearby boundary fence marking the end of the National Trust's Bulkeley Woods. The path curves to the right around a covered reservoir and drops downhill through a plantation of tall larch and Scots pines. At the foot of the slope, keep ahead through a kissing-gate signposted to 'Rawhead' and 'Larkton Hill'.

(For a short detour to the Bickerton Poacher pub, 0.5 kilometre below on the main A534, turn left before the gate on a lesser path through the trees, and go through the metal kissing-gate ahead; then follow the paths shown on the Ordnance Survey map.)

Distant views *Sweeping panoramas open out from the Droppingstone and Rawhead, across the Dee Valley to the distant Welsh mountains*

The Trail heads diagonally across a large field to a T-junction on Coppermines Lane where a fingerpost points straight ahead to 'Rawhead' and 'Whitchurch'. A milestone on the verge opposite reads: 'Coppermine Lane – Frodsham 33km – Whitchurch 22km'. A Sandstone Trail information board shows a route map, local walks, and other useful information.

Go straight ahead on the well-used farm track towards **Rawhead Farm** 64. When the lane bends to the left beyond 'The Bungalow', continue ahead on a broad footpath signposted towards 'Rawhead'.

Within 50 metres, turn left, through a waymarked kissing-gate, and then bear right through scrubby woodland on a path that traverses the contours of the slope. Beyond a small overgrown **quarry** 65, the path rises obliquely across the tree-clad slope. On a clear day, excellent views open out through the trees to the north, back along the sandstone ridge—with Peckforton and Beeston Castles picturesquely aligned on their respective wooded hills. Continue uphill past occasional sandstone outcrops and then skirt beneath a prominent rock overhang.

Roughly 100 metres beyond the overhang, down steep wooden steps on the right, are the ruins of the **Droppingstone Well** 66, on land belonging to the Bolesworth Estate.

Shortly afterwards, the path bends sharply to the left around the end of the escarpment, hugging the corner of the wire fence. Suddenly, the ground falls away to the west and the path climbs crude steps cut into the rock along the lip of a sheer sandstone bluff.

Hidden in the cliffs 50 metres below is a cave called the **Queen's Parlour** 67. (This impressive cavern is on private property. Immediately *before* the bend, illicit visitors have created a faint path that drops down the steep slope before curving around to the left, below the cliff face.)

Beyond a garage-sized detached sandstone block, known locally as the 'Moving Rock' (it has slipped imperceptibly downhill over the last fifty or so years), the Trail rises to a snout-shaped table rock jutting from the cliff top.

Enjoy the view and then continue along the rim of the steep, tree-clad slopes. Ignore a lesser path that drops down steps to the right. Roughly 500 metres later, the path rises to the white-painted, concrete Ordnance Survey triangulation point on the summit of **Rawhead** 68—at 227 metres/ 745 feet above sea level, the highest point on the Trail. The striking panorama spans

Peckforton Gap Lodge around 1910

Still cobbled in parts, **Hill Lane** 59 (also known as the 'Elephant Track') is an ancient packhorse route and salters' way—a short cut over the hills between the Cheshire 'wiches', or salt towns, and the old bridges over the Dee to Wales, at Farndon and Chester. John Wesley, the famous itinerant Methodist preacher, often rode this way when he toured the surrounding Cheshire villages in October 1749.

The arched sandstone **gatehouse** 60 beside the Peckforton Gap on Fowler's Bench Lane once led to the top carriage drive along the ridge to Victorian Peckforton Castle. Today, its double doors open onto a public right of way through the trees towards Hill Lane.

Like much of Cheshire's central sandstone ridge, **Bulkeley Hill** 61 was largely open heather and bilberry-clad lowland heath until grazing by cattle and sheep ceased in the 1930s. Long ago, when the bilberries ripened in mid-July, local children were allowed to skip school to gather the purple fruit.

Local children picking bilberries on Bulkeley Hill in the early 1900s

From 1950 to the present day, Bulkeley Hill has provided water to what was originally the Potteries Water Board's 'Peckforton Pumping Station' at the foot of Peckforton Gap. Engineers working on a 'surge regulator' in 1949 constructed the iron railed **narrow gauge tramline** 62 to haul heavy equipment 120 metres/400 feet to the summit at an angle of more than 40 degrees. The track was never used again. In contrast, Peckforton Pumping Station still sends four million gallons of Cheshire water a day the 40 kilometres/25 miles to Stoke on Trent.

'Name Rock' 63 is a natural sandstone platform jutting from the eastern shoulder of Bulkeley Hill. For centuries, this popular viewpoint has given excellent views across the patchwork of the Cheshire Plain towards the Peak District, the Pennines and Cannock Chase.

Aerial photographs taken during the drought summer of 1976 show a possible undefended Neolithic/Bronze Age settlement in the hilltop fields close to **Rawhead Farm** 64. Flint tools, including a superb Bronze Age barbed and tanged flint arrowhead, have been found nearby on Bickerton Hill.

Now overgrown like many others along the Trail, this disused sandstone **quarry** 65 once supplied hand cut sandstone building blocks for use in nearby cottages, farms and field walls. The quality of the sandstone in these small local quarries varies hugely along the Trail—from hard to crumbly—depending on the degree of mineral cementation. Look closely at the quarry faces and you can see the parallel grooves of the iron hand chisels once used to cut the stone.

much of south Cheshire and the Welsh hills to the west, with the Pennines to the east. Before walking on, take a quick look at the series of smaller caves immediately below Rawhead. The largest is said to have been the home of brigands and was known locally as 'Bloody Bones' cave.

Beyond the 'trig' point, the path veers left and runs on along the lip of the slope. Within 200 metres, turn right, down a long flight of sandstone and timber steps above a deep combe. The path falls gently along the brink of sheer sandstone cliffs to a fenced promontory crowned by pines, above Musket's Hole.

Bear left, and continue past another, permissive, side path down to the right. Roughly 100 metres later, the Trail rises to a southwest-facing sandstone outcrop and viewpoint, with the Bickerton Hills clear in the middle-distance.

Nature Notes

Buzzards have recently overtaken kestrels as Britain's most common bird of prey. Yet until the 1990s, they were seldom seen in Cheshire and the only nesting pairs on this side of the county were on the Duke of Westminster's Eaton Estate, south of Chester. Today, buzzards breed across Cheshire and regularly soar above the hills and woods along the Sandstone Trail. Walkers are almost certain to either see or hear them: watch for large brown birds circling on warm air currents with their wings held in a shallow 'V', or perched, large and upright on a post or branch. Listen, too, for the buzzard's distinctive, far-reaching *pee-oo* cry.

Cheshire Plain *Wide views from Rawhead across the Cheshire Plain towards North Wales*

The path undulates through open birch woods along the upper edge of the slope. Continue above rhododendron-infested Coomb Dale and climb uphill to **Tower Wood** 69. Over the crest of the hill, the Trail hugs the field boundary beside a plantation of mature Scots pines, now with fine views to the east.

Follow the path downhill and go through a kissing-gate beside Chiflik Farm. Just to the northeast here, close to the main road below, is a stone **pumphouse chimney** 70—the sole relic of the area's long copper mining history. Continue ahead on the broad farm drive, and follow it downhill to the right to merge with a narrow, tarmacked lane. The lane levels out, 250 metres later, at a junction with the main A534 Wrexham-Nantwich road—also known as Salters Lane or **Walesmonsway** 71. The area immediately to the east is called **Gallantry Bank** 72.

Cross the busy road with extreme care.

Originally called the 'dripping stone', the **Droppingstone Well** 66 has provided water for nearby farms and cottages since time immemorial. Now partially collapsed, the twin pillared rock overhang and natural spring was once the focus of several paths used daily by local people each carrying a yoke with two buckets or watering cans on their shoulders.

This old postcard shows local paths converging at the Droppingstone Well around 1910

The **Queen's Parlour** 67 is a spectacular, three-chambered cave excavated over the centuries by enterprising people scraping out its soft pale sand. The silver sand was sold to nearby farms from a donkey-drawn cart and used for scouring clean cottage floors, milk churns and cheese-making equipment.

Rawhead 68 is the highest point on the Sandstone Trail at 227 metres/746 feet above sea level. In her 1834 diary a Tattenhall rector's daughter, probably fancifully, described the small caves below the modern Ordnance Survey triangulation point as 'Bloody Bones Caves, the haunt of brigands'.

Ruined copper mine buildings at Bickerton, around 1910

Pedlar and packhorse on the old saltway

Planted with Scots and Corsican pines just before the First World War, in 1913, **Tower Wood** 69 takes its name from long-since vanished, 19th century Horton's Tower, an 'old tower or luncheon room, used by sportsmen during the grouse shooting season'.

A mineralised geological fault runs along the eastern flank of the Peckforton and Bickerton hills. Copper ore was first mined north of Gallantry Bank in 1697. Six shafts were sunk and mining continued intermittently until the 1920s. The **pumphouse chimney** 70 is all that's left after the Victorian mine buildings were demolished by the Bolesworth Estate during the winter of 1928-9.

The modern A534 Wrexham-Nantwich road is known locally as Salters Lane. Previously called 'Walchmonstreet' or **Walesmonsway** 71, it was a 'route for the trade in salt between the Cheshire 'wiches' and Wales'. Packhorses and, later, horse-drawn carts carried salt west into Wales. Travelling eastwards came coal from the North Wales' coalfield to fire the saltpans at Northwich, Nantwich and Middlewich.

Gallantry Bank 72 was originally called Gallows' Tree Bank. The body of a local man named Holford hung for stabbing a rival was gibbeted here in 1640. A few years later, on 19th March 1645, during the Civil War, Prince Rupert had twelve Royalist mutineers summarily strung up from the branches of a nearby crab apple tree.

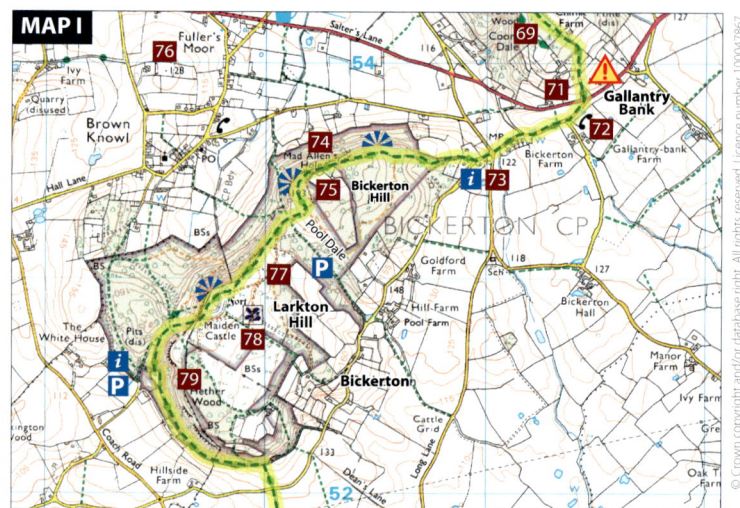

MAP I Across the main road, continue down the quiet lane opposite, signposted to 'Whitchurch'. Walk downhill, past Clay Lane, to Long Lane. Cross Long Lane and continue up Goldford Lane, between **Bickerton Church** 73 and its extended graveyard.

Less than 50 metres on, turn right opposite the Old Vicarage up a path at the rear of a small parking area, signposted to 'Larkton Hill' and 'Whitchurch'. A Trail information board here contains a map, directions, and other useful information.

Go through a waymarked kissing-gate into the woods on the National Trust's 'Bickerton Hill'. A milestone beside the gate says: 'Bickerton – Frodsham 37 km, Whitchurch 18km'.

For the next 0.5 kilometre, the path winds gently uphill through open birch, oak and rowan woodland on Bird's Hill. Beyond a shallow, disused quarry, go through a second gate. As the path ascends, look to the right for occasional glimpses through the trees back to Rawhead and the surrounding hills.

Close to the top, the path dips beside an eroded sandstone bluff; a short scramble down the steep slope to the right here leads to **Mad Allen's Hole** 74, a small cave once occupied by a hermit.

Section five: Burwardsley to Larkton Hall 99

Within 100 metres, the path emerges onto now rare, open lowland heath dominated by heather and bilberries. Stand on the natural table rock beside a touching memorial known as **Kitty's Stone** 75 and enjoy the breezy panorama. The low-lying area at the foot of the slope is called **Fullers Moor** 76. To the north is Rawhead with the rest of the northern section of the Trail stretching beyond it: Pale Heights, Delamere Forest Park, and Frodsham and Helsby Hills, with the Mersey Basin and Liverpool clear on the horizon.

The path curves to the left around the top of the slope. Ignore lesser paths off to the right, to turn right some 200 metres later, down a broad, sunken track signposted to 'Larkton Hill'.

At the bottom of this sandy track, 50 metres later, keep straight on at the crossroads of paths. Ahead is **Larkton Hill** 77, and the shallow intervening valley is called Pool Dale. The Trail winds on through reclaimed heathland dotted with occasional birches. When the path forks, 100 metres later, bear

Rock overhang *Looking down on the little village of Brown Knowl from the sandstone cliffs near Kitty's Stone, on Bickerton Hill*

right and climb the waymarked sandstone steps ahead. The undulating, rising path now skirts the edge of the escarpment and climbs more steps to a broad area of heather and bilberries dotted with occasional birch and rowan trees.

Beyond a dip, the path rises over two, now barely discernible, earthen ramparts encircling **Maiden Castle** **78**, an Iron Age promontory fort perched on the rim of the escarpment. Once within the hillfort, the path arcs gently to the left around the top of the sandstone bluff. Ahead, a new view opens out to the distant Wrekin, Long Mynd and South Shropshire Hills.

Drop down broad sandstone steps at the hillfort's southern end, and turn immediately right, downhill on a narrow path that snakes through the heather above the scarp. When the path forks, 50 metres on, bear right and climb down steps cut into the rock face. The path falls obliquely down the slope with sandstone crags up to the left. The hill ahead is called Cuckoo Rock.

Back in open birch woodland now, turn left at a junction of paths in a natural saddle between the hills, downhill again on a path signposted to

Panoramic views *A group of walkers pause to admire the broad views from Bickerton Hill across the Dee Valley to the Welsh hills*

'Hampton' and 'Whitchurch'. Beyond a small wooden gate in a boundary fence, continue downhill on a waymarked, sunken path just inside the woodland edge.

At the foot of the slope, the path meets a curving track beside a Sandstone Trail information board. (Downhill to the right here is a National Trust car park in a former sandpit. In the early days, when the Trail stretched only 25 kilometres/16 miles from Delamere to Duckington, this was its southern end.) Turn left along the path, above a field, signposted to 'Willeymoor' and 'Whitchurch'.

For the next 800 metres, the path curves around the base of **Hether Wood 79**. Ignore a dedicated horse path rising to the left, and continue above a handful of cottages hedged with dark hollies. Mature oak and holly dominate the densely wooded slopes up to the left, with open fields to the right.

Soon, the path rises gently. Towards the crest of the slope, turn right, through a waymarked kissing-gate, above Larkton Hall Farm. The path descends the sloping field to a kissing-gate into a lane at the foot of the hill.

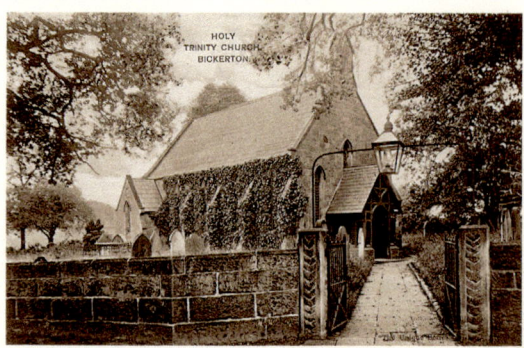
Bickerton church around 1900, still with the old porch

Until 1843, Bickerton was part of the huge parish of Malpas with its 25 townships. Dedicated to the Holy Trinity, **Bickerton Church** **73** was built by public subscription in 1839 as a 'chapel of ease' for local parishioners who for decades had been obliged to walk into Malpas every Sunday—a round trip of 13 kilometres/8 miles or more.

Now partially fallen in, **Mad Allen's Hole** **74** is a two-storey cave, complete with a stone shelf and chimney, once occupied by heartbroken John Harris of Handley. According to a contemporary newspaper, 'About the year 1809, a hermit was discovered in Allenscombe Cave, where he had secreted himself, as he had previously done in a similar cave near to Carden Cliff.'

A generous donation by a bereaved husband in 1991 helped The National Trust buy the northern end of Bickerton Hill. A planned 6 metre/20 foot high stone commemorative obelisk was later modified to a simple sandstone block featuring a poem and photograph. Known simply as **Kitty's Stone** **75**, the two tonne Cumbrian sandstone memorial looks out towards the distant Welsh hills.

Excavations at Maiden Castle in 1934-5 uncovered massive ramparts

The large, low-lying peaty area at the base of the western scarp around Brown Knowl is known as **Fullers Moor** 76. This broad, triangular basin of fertile dark soil was formed on the floor of a pre-glacial lake, which subsequently spilled over, creating the modern gap through the ridge at Gallantry Bank.

'Kitty's Stone' overlooking Brown Knowl

The National Trust cares for 115 hectares/283 acres of mixed woodland and heath on Bickerton Hill and **Larkton Hill** 77. Although land around Maiden Castle was legally 'enclosed' in 1742, the shallow sandy soil ensured that almost the whole hilltop remained as open, treeless heath for centuries. Occasional 'intakes' show where both squatters and farmers have reclaimed land as recently as 1975. Today this rare fragment of lowland heath is managed for both people and wildlife.

Maiden Castle 78 is the southernmost of the severn prehistoric defended settlements along Cheshire's central sandstone ridge. Built by Iron Age farmers around 600BC, the 0.5 hectare/1¼ acre promontory fort is protected by a ditch and double earthen ramparts faced originally with drystone walling. Excavations in 1934-5 uncovered an inturned entrance with guard chambers to the north but few finds. As the hillfort's name implies, it was 'virgin' or untaken.

Hether Wood 79 is a designated Site of Biological Importance. The mature oaks and hollies shelter bats, badgers and owls—and, more particularly, redstarts. Many of the cottages below the woods started out as flimsy squatters' homes, thrown up overnight on common land. Earlier settlers left behind a fine Bronze Age stone axe hammer, subsequently ploughed up on the slopes of Hill Field in September 1975.

Section 6: Larkton Hall to Willeymoor Lock

Distance:	6 miles/9.5 kilometres
Duration:	Allow 3 hours
Difficulty:	Easy: Gently undulating field paths
Parking:	National Trust car park, Hether Wood, Duckington
Refreshments:	Wheatsheaf Inn, No Man's Heath; Willeymoor Lock Tavern, Willeymoor

Outline: *Rolling Cheshire farmland: flooded sand quarries, old coach road, Bickley Brook, subsidence pool, Roman diploma, lost chapel in the fields, ancient inn, ice contact slope, pre-glacial lake bed.*

MAP J Cross the narrow lane at the foot of Larkton Hill and go through the kissing-gate opposite, up the back drive to **Larkton Hall** 80. Continue through the gate 200 metres on and turn right, before the farmyard, through a kissing-gate signposted for the Sandstone Trail.

The path skirts the farm to the west. Head diagonally across the first field, to a waymarked kissing-gate in the far corner. Bear left through the gate and continue straight ahead down the next field, parallel with the farm buildings.

▲ *Larkton Hall*

***Section six:** Larkton Hall to Willeymoor Lock* 105

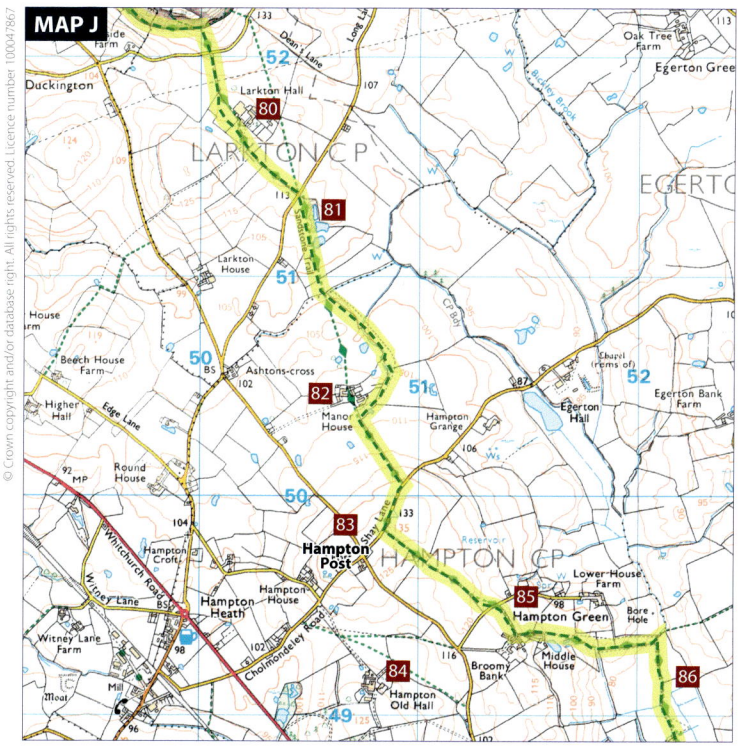

Go through the kissing-gate at the bottom of the field, out onto the main tarmacked drive. Turn right, and walk down the drive to join Long Lane, ahead.

Cross Long Lane to the kissing gate opposite, signposted to 'Hampton Post'. Bear right, along the lefthand edge of the field above three, scrub-shrouded, **flooded sand quarries** 81. Beyond the pools, continue across two large undulating fields and cross a simple footbridge above a ditch.

Ahead is a broad oval of white-railed 'gallops' belonging to Manor House Farm racing stables. Go through the gap in the rails and follow the hedgeline uphill. For the next 750 metres, the regularly waymarked Trail skirts to the east of Manor House Farm. Beyond a kink in the hedge and a Sandstone Trail marker post, the path continues straight ahead at the junction of three large, old fields.

Keep to the left of the willow-fringed pond, and continue up the righthand edge of the large field ahead, with a deep stream ditch on the right. Continue through a broad gap in the hedgeline ahead, and follow the field edge, still with the ditch on your right, as it sweeps to the right around black-and-white **Manor House Farm** 82.

Continue through a gap in more white rails bordering the track to the stables. Almost immediately afterwards, turn right through a kissing-gate in the hedge. Turn immediately left, alongside the hedge and parallel to the wooden stable blocks and roofed exercise ring. Beyond a tiny, tree-fringed pond, go through a waymarked foot gate in the lefthand corner of the field ahead. Turn left and continue uphill beside the hedge to emerge on Shay Lane.

Turn right, and walk uphill on Shay Lane for 250 metres. Over the crest of a rise, turn left through a kissing gate, signposted to 'Bickleywood' and 'Whitchurch'. (Less than 200 metres ahead on Shay Lane is the crossroads

Looking back *Panoramic views of the Bickerton Hills from the summer verges of Shay Lane, near Hampton Post*

at **Hampton Post** 83 —for centuries the site of a well-known staging post on the old coach road.)

From Shay Lane, the Trail heads gently downhill again alongside the hedge. A new panorama opens out ahead, to the east and southeast, across the Cheshire Plain to the distant Pennines and the Peak District. Across the fields to the west is **Hampton Old Hall** 84 one of Cheshire's loveliest early timber-framed houses.

Two fields and 500 metres later, go through a kissing gate beside the hedge and bear left, downhill across two paddocks. Skirt to the left of the wooden stables at the bottom of the slope, and exit into the narrow lane to Lower House Farm. Cross the lane and continue down the tarmacked drive directly opposite to Middle House Farm, signposted to 'Bickleywood' and 'Willeymoor'. Together, this small group of farms comprise the ancient hamlet of **Hampton Green** 85.

Just before the high metal gates of Middle House Farm, 200 metres further on, turn left, off the drive, through a waymarked kissing-gate. Drop down the field boundary to a waymarked foot gate close to a corrugated iron barn. Skirt the barn and follow the high evergreen hedge down to a kissing gate.

Through the kissing gate, bear left, diagonally downhill across the pasture to a footbridge above a ditch. (Ignore a side path across nearby wildflower meadows.) Now turn left and follow the field boundary gently uphill. Over a rise, the path continues straight ahead across a huge undulating field, to a private tractor bridge spanning **Bickley Brook** 86.

Turn left before the bridge and walk along the bank to a dedicated footbridge, less than 30 metres upstream. Over the bridge, turn right, downstream alongside Bickley Brook. Cross a ditch on a short footbridge. Follow the brook downstream for the next 300 metres. When the stream bends sharply to the left, continue straight ahead over a wooden footbridge and almost immediately go through a kissing gate signposted to 'Grindley Brook' and 'Whitchurch'.

Nature Notes

As recently as the 1930s, more than half of Cheshire's farmland was traditional permanent pasture untouched by the plough. Cattle rather than cultivation lay at the heart of local farming. Flower-rich grassland and the wildlife it supports—including specialised insects, brown hares, grey partridges, lapwings and other animals—flourished across Cheshire. Yet since the Second World War Cheshire has lost a staggering 99% of its 'unimproved' grassland to modern intensive agriculture. Fewer than 860 hectares of this declining habitat were left by 1997. Today, Cheshire farmers are recreating 'unimproved' flower meadows, unploughed field edges and hedges under government Stewardship schemes.

Oak dotted pastures *Walkers on the Sandstone Trail cross undulating farmland above Bickley Brook, near No Man's Heath*

Turn left and follow the hedgeline along the upper margin of a large, low-lying, rushy field. At the far end, continue through a kissing gate beside a field gate and walk ahead, uphill, now with a hedge on the right.

When the hedgeline bends sharply to the right, head straight across the pasture towards a metal gate beside a pond in the far corner. Exit onto Bickley Lane. The area west of the brook here is called **Bickleywood** **87**. A Sandstone Trail milestone on the roadside verge reads: 'Bickleywood—Frodsham 45km—Whitchurch 10km'.

Duckington's **Larkton Hall** 80 has a typical Victorian farm layout with buildings arranged around a rectangular central yard. On three sides were the shippon (or milking parlour), stables, tack room, piggeries, grain store and threshing floor—with the cheese parlour on the cooler north side. Until the formation of the Milk Marketing Board in the 1930s, most of the milk from southwest Cheshire's famous dairy herds was made into cheese.

Making traditional Cheshire farmhouse cheese

The southern end of the Sandstone Trail between Larkton Hall and Whitchurch follows a ridge of sand and glacial debris—called a terminal moraine—formed towards the end of the last Ice Age. The overgrown ponds here are **flooded sand quarries** 81, dug originally to extract the thick layers of sand dumped by the retreating ice sheet.

Now run as large-scale racing stables by England footballer Michael Owen and his wife, **Manor House Farm** 82 was the first Cheshire dairy farm to produce bottled Tuberculin Tested milk. Archaeologists suggest the pool beside the Trail immediately to the east of the farm may be a medieval moated site.

Hampton Post 83 was a well-known hilltop staging post and inn on the old London to Chester coach road. As roads improved, journey times shortened. Eighteenth-century travel writer

The post office at No Man's Heath, around 1910

Thomas Pennant's journey from London to Chester took six days in 1739. When the new turnpike—the modern A41—was finished in 1821, a stagecoach called the Manchester Telegraph covered the 290 kilometre/180 mile trip in a record eighteen hours and fifteen minutes.

Solid gold Bronze Age 'Malpas torc' and armlets from Hampton Green

Built in 1591 but much altered and extended, **Hampton Old Hall** 84 is one of Cheshire's loveliest black-and-white Elizabethan mansions. While the front sports three timber-framed gables with distinctive balustrade-shaped decoration, the servants' wing to the rear is constructed of brick and stone with mullioned windows. Originally the family seat of the Bromleys, the hall was later bought by the Willding-Jones's. During the 1990s, the grounds were the venue for the annual Malpas Yesteryear Rally featuring a complete steam fairground and scores of traction engines.

A group of farms make up the isolated ancient hamlet of **Hampton Green** 85. Its communal 'green'—like those at Yarrangal Green, near Alvanley, and Fishers Green, near Tarporley—was enclosed in 1829. That same year, workmen digging the foundations for a new cottage nearby uncovered two beautiful Bronze Age twisted gold armlets and a gold necklace, or torc, now displayed in the Manchester Museum.

Bickley Brook 86 is a narrow stream in a broad valley carved originally by glacial meltwaters towards the close of the last Ice Age. Its unpolluted waters provide ideal habitat for otters, small fish, freshwater shrimps and the rare native white-clawed crayfish. Protected by a DEFRA stewardship scheme, green plovers (also known as 'peewits' or lapwings) nest on the streamside water meadows.

Now rolling, open farmland, **Bickleywood** 87 was once clothed in extensive woodland according to a seventeenth-century map. Clues to a possible deserted medieval village at Bickley appear on modern aerial photographs; and a first century Roman silver ring was discovered in a field at nearby Robberhill, close to the old coach road.

Ancient chapel *Old St Chad's Chapel, near Tushingham, cannot be reached by road*

MAP K From the milestone at Bickleywood, turn right, past a lay-by, along Bickley Lane for 100 metres; then turn left down a narrow lane.

(Alternatively, for refreshments, continue on along Bickley Lane for just under a kilometre and cross the main A41 ⚠ into No Man's Heath.)

Less than 150 metres later, turn left, off the lane, through a waymarked metal kissing gate. Then turn right through another kissing gate and head out across the undulating pasture, parallel with Bickley Hall Farm (now the headquarters of the Cheshire Wildlife Trust), to a waymarker post on the crest of the slope ahead. At the bottom of the slope, go through a metal footgate beside the field gate.

Follow the fence and hedgeline for 200 metres ahead and turn right through a waymarked kissing gate. Bear diagonally to the left, to a waymarker at the corner of the hedge. Turn left around the corner, and then bear right, diagonally across the field to a waymarker post on the crest of the slope. Continue to a kissing gate beside a field gate in the far hedgeline, below. (Interestingly, one field away, some 250 metres to the south-west, is a tree-lined pool called **Barhill Fall** 88 —created in a few violent minutes in 1657.)

Once through the kissing gate, follow the fenceline across the small, oddly

Section six: Larkton Hall to Willeymoor Lock 113

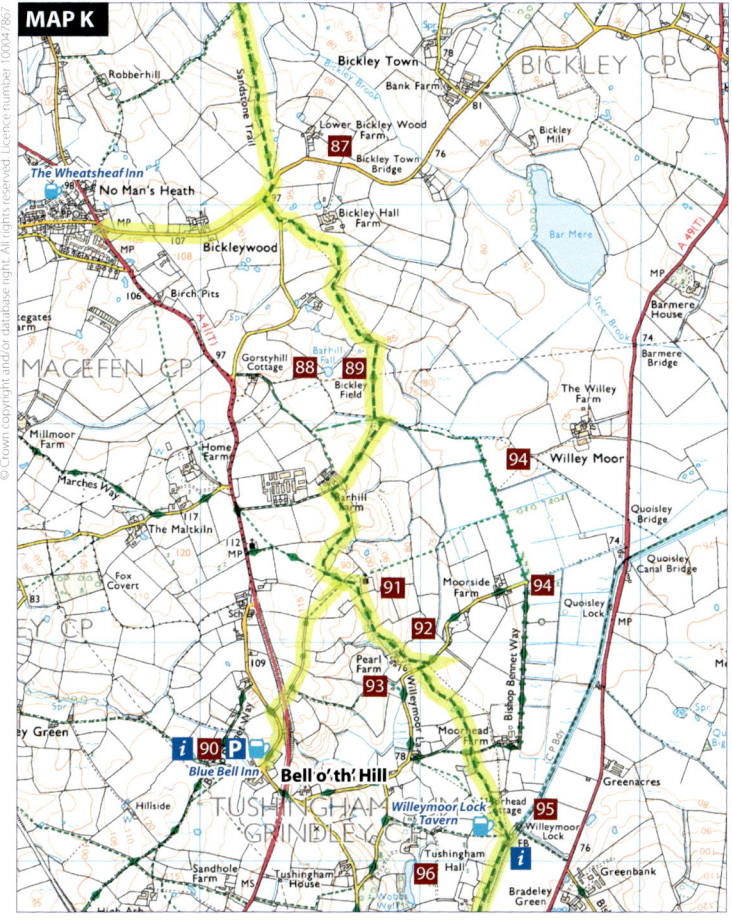

shaped field ahead, and turn right, 30 metres later, through another kissing gate. Keeping close to the hedge, walk along the righthand edge of the large, undulating field.

(Pause beneath the power lines halfway along, and look to the right across the adjacent Bickley Field. Not far from here the fascinating **'Malpas Roman Diploma'** 89 was discovered by Victorian ditchers.)

Continue along the hedgeline and drop down to a waymarker beside a gate in the bottom righthand corner of the field. Go straight ahead, uphill on a broad farm track towards white-painted Barhill Farm. (Ignore the bridleway that crosses the Trail at the base of the slope.)

At the top of the track, go through the gate into the farmyard. Walk straight through the yard, keeping an eye out for working agricultural machinery. Turn left through a kissing gate immediately opposite Barhill Farmhouse.

Follow the fenceline across the field, and go through a waymarked kissing gate in the far corner, 150 metres later. Bear left, along the fence, and continue through another kissing gate 50 metres on.

Turn right, and cross the top of the sloping field to a waymarked kissing gate in the hedgeline opposite. Follow the hedge as it curves around to the left, and leave through the waymarked gate hidden in the field corner. (From here, the Sandstone Trail shares its route with the Marches Way for a while).

Lost church? *Old St Chad's Chapel is hidden in the fields close to the Sandstone Trail*

(For a short detour to the now closed, Grade II listed **Blue Bell Inn** 90 —once one of Cheshire's oldest pubs—turn right and go through the gate at the top of the large field, then follow Chad Lane across the main A49 ⚠ to the hamlet of Bell o' th' Hill.)

Hidden by dark yews and cedars, across the field, is the curious and isolated **Old St Chad's Chapel** 91. It's well worth a closer look. The Trail continues over a waymarked kissing gate in the hedge immediately to the right of the chapel grounds, signposted to 'Willeymoor' and 'Whitchurch'.

Head straight down the field to a waymarked kissing gate at the bottom of the slope. The steep hillside that curves around below St Chad's is an **Ice Contact Slope** 92, formed at the end of the last Ice Age. Through the gate, bear slightly to the right and follow the grassy hollow way downhill to a waymarked kissing gate immediately to the left of black-and-white **Pearl Farm** 93, below.

Past the duckpond, walk down the drive and turn left through the kissing gate. Cross the paddock to another kissing gate in the far corner and turn

Canalside pub *Boaters navigate the lock outside the Willeymoor Lock Tavern on the Llangollen arm of the Shropshire Union Canal*

sharp right, along Willeymoor Lane. Turn left, almost immediately, over a ditch on a crude footbridge signposted to 'Willeymoor Lock'.

The low-lying, peaty area to the east is a pre-glacial lake floor represented today by **Willeymoor** 94, Barmere and Quoisley Meres. Follow the hedgeline and a series of waymarked kissing gates across the next three fields. Cross the lane to Moorhead Farm, and then follow the paling fence alongside the drive to thatched Moorhead Cottage, ahead.

Go through a gate and cross the drive to a waymarked kissing gate to the right of Moorhead Cottage. Walk across the field to another gate to the right of white-painted Willeymoor Lock Tavern, ahead. Continue alongside the beer garden and go up steps onto the towpath of the **Llangollen Canal** 95 at Willeymoor Lock.

Nature Notes

Increasingly rare brown hares can still be seen in the open farmland around St Chad's Chapel and across low-lying Willeymoor. Intensive farming and changes in land use since the Second World War have led to an alarming decline of this once common species. The British brown hare population peaked at around four million in Victorian times but decreased substantially from the 1950s to the 1980s; nationally, numbers today may be as low as 800,000. Interestingly, a questionnaire sent to 4,000 local farms in 2000 puts the Cheshire hare population at around 6,100. The main threats to brown hares today are habitat loss and poaching.

Roman 'Malpas Diploma', now in the British Museum, London

The curious **Barhill Fall** 88 is now an apparently unremarkable tree-encircled pool. But until 8th July 1657 it was an oak-topped hillock. A contemporary witness wrote: 'A piece of ground 30 yards over fell in with a huge noise and great oaks growing on it fell in together. Out of which pit they drew brine with a pitcher tied to a cart rope but could find no bottom...

Now preserved in the British Museum in London, the two-part hinged bronze **'Malpas Roman Diploma'** 89 was uncovered by ditchers close to Barhill Fall at Tushingham, in 1812. A minor Roman road to Whitchurch (*Mediolanum*) passed nearby. The diploma was issued on the 19th January AD103 and granted citizenship to Reburrus the Spaniard for 25 years army service. Reburrus was a junior cavalry officer—or *decurio*—of the First Pannonian Regiment.

Now closed, the delightful timber-framed **Blue Bell Inn** 90 at Bell o' th' Hill, near Tushingham, was one of Cheshire's oldest pubs. Shown on Ogilby's Britannia Roadbook in 1675 as 'Ye signe of ye bel', it stands beside the old coach road. It's said a ghostly duck that once plagued the pub was exorcised and trapped in a bottle—where it still remains, bricked up in the cellar.

First recorded in a deed of 1349 and built originally of timber, **Old St Chad's Chapel** 91 was rebuilt in 1689-91, and again in 1841. An ancient holy well is

Blue Bell Inn, Bell o' th' Hill, around 1910

mentioned nearby in 1620. The adjoining hearse house holds a horse-drawn 'Black Maria' donated by a retiring vicar in 1891. Special services are held here each year on Ascension Day (forty days after Easter) and Rushbearing Day (the first Sunday in August).

Old St Chad's chapel, Tushingham, around 1900

As the vast ice sheet retreated towards the end of the last Ice Age, there were periods of equilibrium when massive barriers of glacial debris built up called terminal moraines. The steep slope below St Chad's Chapel at Tushingham is the old **Ice Contact Slope** 92 where the *moraine* met the stationary glacier. On the far side of Willeymoor is another parallel but incomplete terminal moraine towards Cholmondeley and Norbury.

Pearl Farm 93 is a pretty timber-framed, brick-nogged farmhouse with mullion windows. A Latin inscription above the door dates it to 1607. As at Pearl Hole near Willington to the north, its curious name probably derives from the spring at the base of the ice-contact slope behind the farm: *pyrle* is Old English for a 'bubbling stream'.

The low-lying, rich peaty ground around **Willeymoor** 94, Barmere and Quoisey Meres represents the floor of a glacial meltwater lake. A reference to 'Tussyncham Ferry' in a deed of 1483 suggests the area may have remained flooded into the Middle Ages. Later, as part of the 18th century trend for Parliamentary Enclosures, 80 hectares/200 acres of former boggy common land or 'waste' on Willeymoor were drained and reclaimed in 1795.

The most popular and probably the loveliest waterway in Britain, the **Llangollen Canal** 95 runs for 74 kilometres/46 miles between Hurleston Junction on the main Shropshire Union Canal and the River Dee, above Llangollen, in North Wales. Essentially a navigable feeder, the canal survived because of its importance as a water supply. Today, the canal offers a perfect week's narrowboating: the round trip to Llangollen and back takes three days each way.

Section 7: Willeymoor Lock to Whitchurch

Distance:	3½ miles/5.5 kilometres
Duration:	Allow 1½-2 hours
Difficulty:	Easy: Level canal towpath, and surfaced town paths
Parking:	There is NO easy parking at Willeymoor Lock, or on the nearby A49. The pub car park is for patrons only and cars should not be left here. The closest alternative parking is opposite the Blue Bell Inn at Bell o' th' Hill
Refreshments:	Willeymoor Lock Tavern, Willeymoor Lock; Horse and Jockey, Grindley Brook; Lockside Café, Grindley Brook Locks; pubs and cafés in Whitchurch

Outline: *Along the Llangollen Canal: old hall, coaching stop, home of Cheshire Blue cheese, staircase locks, former canal-road-rail junction and wharf, rolling farmland, rare 'lift-up' bridge, restored canal arm, Georgian market town.*

MAP L Turn right along the towpath at Willeymoor Lock. (Alternatively, turn left to stop off at the nearby canalside Willeymoor Lock Tavern—known locally as 'The Hole in the Wall'—for food, drink and a friendly welcome.) For the next 4.5 kilometres, the Trail follows the picturesque **Llangollen**

▲ *Willeymoor Lock and pub*

Section seven: Willeymoor Lock to Whitchurch 121

Canal 95 south across open, undulating farmland towards the outskirts of Whitchurch. The final kilometre traces the Whitchurch Arm of the canal into the Georgian town centre.

The Sandstone Trail information board on the towpath near Willeymoor Lock displays maps, a brief route description and other useful information. Some 300 metres to the south is Povey's Lock. The open parkland sprinkled with mature trees on the right belongs to nearby **Tushingham Hall** 96.

Within 0.5 kilometre the towpath passes the curiously-named **Land of Canaan** 97—a white-painted farm at the top of the slope on the right. Continue along the reed-fringed towpath to narrow, brick-built **Jackson's Bridge** 98—(bridge number 26). Several fields away, across the canal to the left, is gastronomically important **Hinton Bank Farm** 99.

Another half kilometre on, the canal bends to the left beneath a disused railway embankment. Notice the Sandstone Trail milestone beside the

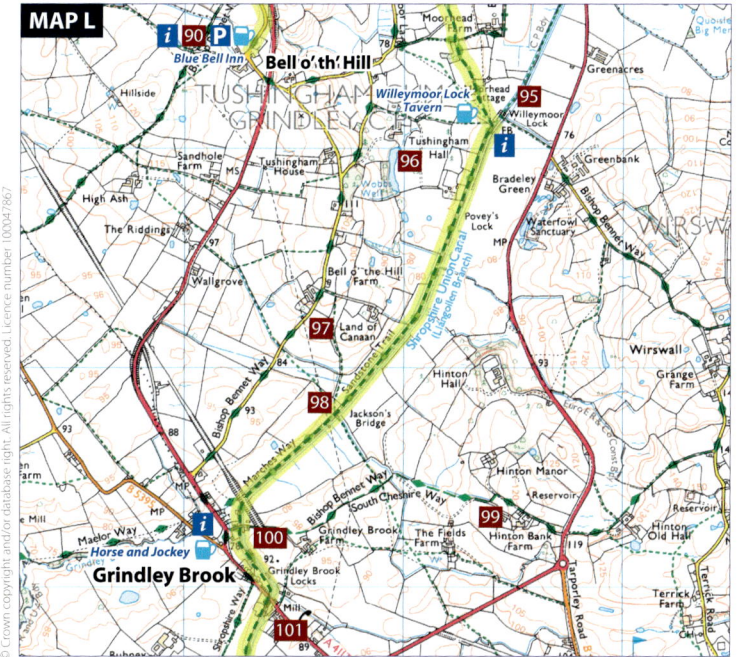

towpath immediately before the brick arch. It reads: 'Grindley Brook – Frodsham 51km – Whitchurch 4km'.

On the far side of the embankment is **Grindley Brook** 100, a small settlement that prospered in the days when it was a busy junction of road, rail and canal. Today, it's the meeting point of several long-distance trails: the Sandstone Trail, Marches Way, South Cheshire Way, Shropshire Way, Maelor Way, and the horse-riders' Bishop Bennet's Way.

Continue along the towpath past a wooden warehouse and under a brick canal bridge. Just after the first of three locks, a gate in the canalside fence leads to a petrol station and well-stocked shop. Across the main A41 opposite is the Horse and Jockey, a 'traditional English pub' that serves 'food daily'.

Follow the towpath gently uphill past two further locks. The canal bends to the right, and passes beneath the busy main road.

Welsh water? *A traditionally-painted water can and narrowboat on the Llangollen arm of the Shropshire Union Canal, near Whitchurch*

Section seven: *Willeymoor Lock to Whitchurch* 123

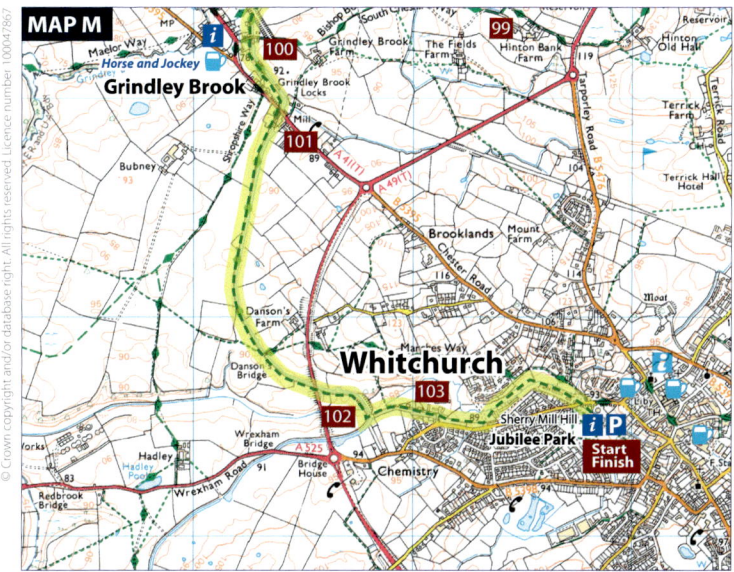

MAP M The flight of three staircase locks beyond the bridge lead up to the now quiet **Grindley Brook Wharf** 101. The potentially tricky locks here originally justified the building of a distinctive round-fronted lock keeper's house at the top. Today the nearby 'Lockside Stores' sells: 'Local farm produce, fresh foods, groceries, beers, wines, and canal gifts'.

For the next kilometre, the canal runs south, past a lonely canalside cottage to whitewashed Danson's Bridge, close to Danson's Farm. Continue along the towpath beneath a modern steel and concrete bridge carrying the A41 Whitchurch by-pass.

Close to Whitchurch now, the canal snakes left and right to the unusual, counterbalanced **New Mills Lift Bridge** 102. Turn left over the bridge to join the recently restored **Whitchurch Canal Arm** 103.

When the canal arm bends to the right, 150 metres later, look over the gate to the left: currently a nature reserve, the stream valley here is earmarked for a bold scheme to canalise Stags Brook, complete with an inclined plane, moorings and a fishing lake. Continue along the towpath past a turning area for narrowboats known as a 'winding hole'.

Flag day? *Medieval black-and-white and Georgian brick buildings*

At the end of the canal arm is the original though much-restored, handmade brick Chemistry Bridge. Continue straight ahead beneath a reinforced concrete road bridge, and follow the surfaced path across open ground to the road ahead.

Cross the road and turn left. Almost immediately, go down steps on the right, signposted for the 'Sandstone Trail' and 'Town'. Bear right and follow the surfaced and waymarked path that runs parallel to Stag Brook along the valley. Ignore a side path to the left, signposted to 'Danson's Farm', and continue straight ahead across the end of a residential cul-de-sac.

The path is signposted for the 'Sandstone Trail' and 'Town'. Continue on the surfaced path beyond another side path to 'Chester Road'. Bear right, and cross the footbridge over Stag Brook to emerge almost immediately in Waterside Close. Keep straight ahead and cross Sherry Mill Hill Road to Sherry Mill Hill Car Park, at the western end of Jubilee Park, directly opposite. An arch of sandstone blocks celebrates the southern end of the Sandstone Trail.

The car park is situated not far from the centre of Whitchurch.

(For the town centre, turn left, and walk up Sherry Mill Hill towards the prominent tower of St Alkmund's Church.)

Nature Notes

Otters are making a welcome comeback across Britain. The Llangollen Canal provides an essential wildlife corridor along which Welsh otters are now recolonising the border counties of Shropshire and Cheshire. Plentiful evidence of resident otters—in the form of fresh footprints and their distinctive droppings, or 'spraints'—has been found along the Chemistry stretch of the Whitchurch Arm and nearby Stags Brook, on the very edge of Whitchurch. Otters are largely nocturnal and need secure resting places, or 'holts', to lie up in by day. So sensitive canal and river management and habitat conservation are vital if our English otters are to flourish.

Already called 'an ancient manor house' as far back as 1650, **Tushingham Hall** 96 was extended in the Gothick style, rendered and battlemented in the early 1800s. A house diary and account book for the years 1808-1860 includes: 'syringing Miss Churton's ears 2/6d, applying leeches 2/6d, a gallon of red port 7/6d, cowslip wine 1/6d'.

Tushingham Hall seen across the lake, sometime in the late 1800s

The unusually named **Land of Canaan** 97 farm first appears on the hand-inked Tithe Maps of 1838. The name refers to the biblical 'Promised Land' with which God rewarded Abraham's obedience. The farmhouse was reputedly a popular staging post and inn on the old coach road during the eighteenth century.

For two centuries farm animals and local workers have crossed the Llangollen Canal on narrow, handmade brick-built **Jackson's Bridge** 98. Now the bridge provides a welcome shortcut across the fields to the South Cheshire Way and Hinton Bank Farm.

Originally called Cheshire Stilton, Cheshire Blue Vein cheese was first developed and marketed by cheese factor Geoffrey Hutchinson of the

New Mills Lift bridge with fishermen around 1910

Hampton Post Inn in 1902. Today this famous cheese is still made at **Hinton Bank Farm** 99, a kilometre/¾ mile or so to the east of Grindley Brook.

Grindley Brook 100 is the meeting point of road, rail and canal. The modern A41 follows the route of the old Roman road between Chester (*Deva*) and Whitchurch (*Mediolanum*); when the road was turnpiked in 1759, a tollgate was set up between the canal bridge and the Horse and Jockey pub. The railway line from Chester to Whitchurch closed in 1963. Yet the canal is kept alive by growing numbers of leisure boaters.

Six locks were necessary on this short 0.8 kilometre/½ mile stretch of the Llangollen Canal, completed in 1805. At the top of the three lock staircase immediately to the west of the A41 is **Grindley Brook Wharf** 101. Nearby are a disused corn mill and the old Grindley Brook Hotel—at one time a staging post on the old coach road and a rowdy canalside tavern.

Lift bridges are the cheapest and simplest way of crossing a canal and were common on rural waterways. Made to a conventional design, the **New Mills Lift Bridge** 102 beside the Whitchurch Arm uses a weight box at the far end of the overhead arms to counterbalance the weight of the bridge. This allows the bridge to be raised to a high angle, giving good clearance for passing boats.

The Llangollen Canal simply bypassed Whitchurch until angry townspeople campaigned for the **Whitchurch Canal Arm** 103—which opened in 1808. New wharves in the centre of town prospered for decades. But, after years of decline, the Arm was finally closed in 1944, and filled in on safety grounds during the 1950s. In a bold initiative, the Whitchurch Waterway Trust reopened the Canal Arm in October 1993.

Whitchurch High Street before the First World War

Useful Information

For more information about the **Sandstone Trail**, including how to get there, where to stay, where to eat, local attractions, events, geology, history, wildlife, photo gallery, competition, other Cheshire walks, and much more, see the comprehensive dedicated website:

www.sandstonetrail.co.uk